Remember This?

People, Things and Events
FROM **1946** TO THE **PRESENT DAY**

US EDITION

All product names and brands are property of their respective owners. No endorsement is given or implied.

With thanks for additional research by Larry Farr, Dana Lemay, Rose Myers and Idan Solon.

Baby statistics: Office of Retirement and Disability Policy, Social Security Administration.

Cover: Mary Evans: LANL/Science Source, Everett Collection, Keystone Pictures USA/zumapress.com; Library of Congress: FSA/OWI Collection LC-DIG-fsa-8a04542. Icons from rawpixel/Freepik.

Cover Design: Fanni Williams / thehappycolourstudio.com

The Milestone Memories series including this *Remember This?* title is produced by Milestones Memories Press, a division of Say So Media Ltd.

First edition: October 2021
Updated: February 2022

We've tried our best to check our facts, but mistakes can still slip through. Spotted one? We'd love to know about it: info@saysomedia.net

Rewind, Replay, Remember

What can you remember before you turned six? If you're like most of us, not much: the comforting smell of a blanket or the rough texture of a sweater, perhaps. A mental snapshot of a parent arriving home late at night. A tingle of delight or the shadow of sorrow.

But as we grow out of childhood, our autobiographical and episodic memories—they're the ones hitched to significant events such as birthdays or leaving school—are created and filed more effectively, enabling us to piece them together at a later date. And the more we revisit those memories, the less likely we are to lose the key that unlocks them.

We assemble these fragments into a more-or-less coherent account of our lives—the one we tell to ourselves, our friends, our relatives. And while this one-of-a-kind biopic loses a little definition over the years, some episodes remain in glorious technicolor—although it's usually the most embarrassing incidents!

But this is one movie that's never quite complete. Have you ever had a memory spring back unbidden, triggered by something seemingly unrelated? This book is an attempt to discover those forgotten scenes using the events, sounds, and faces linked to the milestones in your life.

It's time to blow off the cobwebs and see how much you can remember!

It Happened in 1946

The biggest event in the year is one that didn't make the front pages: you were born! Here are some of the national stories that people were talking about.

- Basketball Association of America formed
- Bank with 10 drive-up teller windows opens
- B.B. King's first live performance
- Truman establishes President's Committee on Civil Rights
- St. Louis Cardinals win the World Series
- Dean Martin & Jerry Lewis stage their first show as a team
- Telephone for a car demonstrated
- Bill Haley's career begins
- The Philippines granted independence
- Mother Frances Xavier Cabrini canonized
- United Mine Workers joins with American Federation of Labor
- Tupperware invented
- Central Intelligence Group established
- It's a Wonderful Life released
- Aleutian Islands earthquake
- Hawaii struck by tidal waves
- Benjamin Spock's childcare book published
- US begins atomic testing on Bikini Atoll (right)
- United Nations meets

Born this year:
- Donald Trump
- George W. Bush
- Bill Clinton
- Singer Dolly Parton

Nine months after atomic bombs were dropped on Hiroshima and Nagasaki, Operation Crossroads tested the effect of nuclear weapons on warships. Held in the Bikini Atoll, the first test, Able, detonated in the air above the target ships (the 1945 bombs were also "air bursts"). Although only 5 of the 90-strong fleet were sunk, many more were showered in fatal but temporary doses of radiation. The second test, Baker (shown above), detonated 90 feet below water. It sank more ships and showered the fleet in radioactive spray. Live animals were positioned on board to gauge radiation, and more than 42,000 personnel were engaged in the tests and the subsequent cleanup.

On the Bookshelf When You Were Small

The books of our childhood linger long in the memory. These are the children's classics, all published in your first ten years. Do you remember the stories? What about the covers?

1946	**Thomas the Tank Engine by Rev. W. Awdry** Rev. Awdrey appeared in his own books as the Thin Clergyman. His more portly friend in real life, Teddy Boston, appeared by his fictional side—known, of course, as the Fat Clergyman.
1946	Scuffy the Tugboat by Gertrude Crampton
1946	**The Mystery of the Tolling Bell by Carolyn Keene** The Nancy Drew series ran for 175 books. The author of the early titles was adventurer journalist Mildred Wirt Benson. She received a flat fee and no recognition until a 1980 court case unraveled her contribution.
1947	Goodnight Moon by Margaret Wise Brown
1948	My Father's Dragon by Ruth Stiles Gannett
1948	Blueberries for Sal by Robert McCloskey
1949	**Bartholomew and the Oobleck by Dr. Seuss** Oobleck is the atrociously gummy substance that rains from the sky in Dr. Seuss's tale, broadly summarized as "be careful what you wish for." Oobleck lives on as the amazing non-Newtonian liquid made from cornstarch.
1949	Song of the Swallows by Leo Politi
1950	The Lion, the Witch and the Wardrobe by C.S. Lewis
1951	The Wailing Siren Mystery by Franklin W. Dixon
1952	Charlotte's Web by E.B. White
1952	The Borrowers by Mary Norton
1953	...And Now, Miguel by Joseph Krumgold
1954	Cinderella, or the Little Glass Slipper by Marcia Brown
1955	**Harold and the Purple Crayon by Crockett Johnson** The author behind the Harold series was cartoonist David Johnson Leisk. He worked with his wife, Ruth Krauss, on the 1945 bestseller The Carrot Seed, and created geometric paintings which now hang in the National Museum of American History.

Around the World in Your Birth Year

Here are the events from outside the US that were big enough to make news back home in the year you were born. And you won't remember any of them!

- ✦ United Nations meets
- ✦ Bikinis go on sale in France
- ✦ Casio company is founded
- ✦ Swedish PM dies of heart attack
- ✦ Japan grants women the vote
- ✦ UNESCO holds first session
- ✦ League of Nations disbands
- ✦ Churchill makes "Iron Curtain" speech
- ✦ BBC resumes public broadcasts
- ✦ Britain mines are nationalized
- ✦ Jordan wins independence
- ✦ War crimes trials begin in Japan
- ✦ UNICEF is founded
- ✦ Vietnam holds general election
- ✦ Hungary becomes a republic
- ✦ Peron becomes president of Argentina
- ✦ Mensa is founded
- ✦ Italy becomes republic
- ✦ Crisis occurs in Iran
- ✦ Millions die of starvation in China
- ✦ Philippines gains independence
- ✦ War Crime Tribunal sentences Nazis to death
- ✦ Cannes Film Festival begins

Boys' Names When You Were Born

Once upon a time, popular names came… and stuck. (John hogged the top spot for 40 years, to 1924.) These are the most popular names when you were born.

James
James was not only the first choice in 1946, it was the most popular boy's name of the last hundred years, bestowed upon nearly five million babies (narrowly beating John into second place).

Robert
John
William
Richard
David
Michael
Thomas
Charles
Ronald
Larry
Gary
Donald
Joseph
Kenneth
George
Dennis
Paul
Edward
Jerry
Daniel
Frank
Roger
Stephen

Rising and falling stars:
Herbert and Gene made their final Top 100 appearance in 1946; Keith and Rodney made their debut.

Girls' Names When You Were Born

On the girls' side of the maternity ward, Mary and Helen topped the list for decades. But by 1946, Helen had fallen to 36th position and Mary held the crown for the last time...

Mary
Mary was the name chosen for 3 million babies over the last century: twice as many as Patricia, the second most popular pick overall.

Linda
Patricia
Barbara
Carol
Sandra
Nancy
Susan
Sharon
Judith

Judy
11th place was Judy's highest ever ranking.

Carolyn
Donna
Betty
Karen
Kathleen
Margaret
Shirley
Diane
Joyce
Janet
Janice
Dorothy
Brenda

Rising and falling stars:
Carole was 73rd in 1946, but would never be seen again.
Kathy, Lynn, Maureen and Marsha were fresh faces.

Things People Did When You Were Growing Up...

...that hardly anyone does now. Some of these we remember fondly; others are best left in the past!

- ✦ Help Mom make cookies using a cookie press
- ✦ Keep bread in a breadbox
- ✦ Can and preserve vegetables from your garden
- ✦ Listen to daytime soap operas on the radio
- ✦ Participate in Church fundraisers
- ✦ Watch endurance competitions like flagpole sitting and goldfish eating
- ✦ Build scooters from roller skates and scrap wood
- ✦ Bring a slide-rule to math class
- ✦ Take a Sunday drive out to the country
- ✦ Play leapfrog
- ✦ Live in a Sears Modern Home ordered from the Sears catalog
- ✦ Get a treat from the pharmacy soda fountain
- ✦ Camp in a "Hooverville" while looking for work
- ✦ Keep a thrift or kitchen garden
- ✦ Buy penny candy
- ✦ Buy goods from door-to-door salesmen
- ✦ Wear clothing made from flour sacks
- ✦ Collect marbles
- ✦ Join a dance marathon
- ✦ Listen to Amos n' Andy on the radio on weekend evenings
- ✦ Eat Water Pie
- ✦ "Window shop" downtown on Saturdays
- ✦ Pitch pennies
- ✦ Earn $30 a month plus food and shelter working for the Civilian Conservation Corps

How Many of These Games Are Still Played?

The first half of the 20th century was the heyday for new board and card games launched to the US public. Some are still firm family favorites, but which ones did you play when you were young?

1925	Pegity
1925	Playing for the Cup
1927	Hokum ("The game for a roomful")
1920s	The Greyhound Racing Game
1930	Wahoo
1932	Finance
1934	Sorry!
1935	**Monopoly**

The game's origins lie with The Landlord's Game, patented in 1904 by Elizabeth Magie. (The anti-monopoly version—Prosperity—didn't catch on.) It was the first game with a never-ending path rather than a fixed start and finish.

1935	Easy Money
1936	The Amazing Adventures of Fibber McGee
1937	Meet the Missus
1937	Stock Ticker
1938	Scrabble
1938	Movie Millions
1940	Dig
1940	Prowl Car
1942	Sea Raider
1943	Chutes and Ladders
1949	**Clue**

Clue—or Cluedo, as it is known to most outside the USA—introduced us to a host of shady characters and grisly murder weapons. For years those included a piece of genuine lead pipe, now replaced on health grounds.

1949	**Candy Land**

This wholesome family racing game, invented on a polio ward, was the victim of something less savory nearly 50 years after its launch when an adult website claimed the domain name. Thankfully, the courts swiftly intervened.

Things People Do Now...

...that were virtually unknown when you were young. How many of these habits are part of your routine or even second nature these days? Do you remember the first time?

- ✦ Get curbside grocery pickup
- ✦ Stream movies instead of going to Blockbuster for a rental
- ✦ Learn remotely and online
- ✦ Communicate by text or video chat
- ✦ Use a Kindle or other e-reading device
- ✦ Go geocaching
- ✦ Track your sleep, exercise, or fertility with a watch
- ✦ Use a weighted blanket
- ✦ Use a robotic/automatic vacuum
- ✦ Take your dog to a dog park
- ✦ Have a package delivered by drone
- ✦ Find a date online or through an app
- ✦ Use hand sanitizer
- ✦ Automatically soothe your baby with a self-rocking bassinet
- ✦ Host a gender-reveal party during pregnancy
- ✦ Use a home essential oil diffuser or salt lamp
- ✦ Have a "destination wedding"
- ✦ Use a device charging station while waiting for a flight
- ✦ Get a ride from Uber or Lyft instead of a taxi
- ✦ Drink hard seltzer
- ✦ Take a home DNA test (for you... or your pet)
- ✦ Have a telemedicine/virtual healthcare visit
- ✦ Smoke an e-cigarette/"vape"
- ✦ Start your car, dryer, or air conditioner via an app

Popular Food in the 1950s

For many, the post-war years meant more of one thing in particular on the table: meat. In the yard, men stepped up to the barbeque to sharpen their skills. In the kitchen, fancy new electric appliances and frozen TV dinners promised convenience and new, exotic flavors.

Tuna noodle casserole

Dinty Moore Beef Stew

Beef stroganoff

Green bean casserole

Green bean casserole was invented in the Campbell's test kitchen in 1955 as a cheap, fuss-free dish. Today, around 40 percent of Campbell's Cream of Mushroom soup sold in the US goes into this dinner table staple.

Pigs-in-a-blanket

Pigs get different blankets in the United Kingdom, where sausages are wrapped in bacon rather than pastry.

Backyard barbecues

Ovaltine

Swedish meatballs

Pineapple upside down cake

Spam

Ground pork shoulder and ham sold in a distinctive can—for much of the world, that means Spam. This "meatloaf without basic training" is affordable and still popular, with over eight billion cans sold since it was first sold in 1937.

Ambrosia salad

Sugar Smacks

Cheez Whiz

Stuffed celery

Campbell's Tomato Soup spice cake

Swanson Turkey TV Dinners

Dreamed up as a solution to an over-supply of turkey, TV dinners proved nearly as popular as the TV itself. Swanson sold over 25 million of them in 1954, the year these handy meal packs were launched.

Veg-All canned vegetables

Chicken à la King

Cars of the 1950s

Was this the golden age of automobiles? In truth, some of these models had been brought to market long before, such as the Buick Roadmaster and the Studebaker Champion. But even stalwarts were quick to adopt the Space Age theme of the decade as sweeping lines, tailfins, and cascading chrome grilles became the norm.

1926	Chrysler Imperial
1936	General Motors Buick Roadmaster
1939	**Studebaker Champion** Over seven decades, the Champion's creator, Raymond Loewy, designed railroads, logos, buses, vending machines, and a space station for NASA.
1939	Chrysler DeSoto Custom
1947	Studebaker Starlight Coupe
1948	**Crosley Station Wagon** The first car to be marketed as "Sports Utility."
1948	Jaguar XK120
1949	**Muntz Jet** Fewer than 200 Muntz Jets were built by founder Madman Muntz, an engineer who married seven times and made (and lost) fortunes selling cars, TVs, and more.
1949	Chrysler Dodge Coronet
1950	General Motors Chevrolet Bel-Air
1950	Nash Rambler
1951	Hudson Hornet
1953	General Motors Chevrolet Corvette
1953	General Motors Buick Skylark
1953	General Motors Cadillac Eldorado
1953	Nash Metropolitan
1954	Ford Skyliner
1955	Ford Thunderbird
1955	Ford Fairlane
1956	Studebaker Golden Hawk
1956	Chrysler Plymouth Fury
1957	**Mercedes-Benz 300 SL Roadster** Voted "Sports Car of the Century" in 1999.

Cars crawl out of 1950s Philadelphia over the Ben Franklin Bridge. Henry Ford wasn't the only one to "build a car for the great multitude." Millions of new suburbanites embraced their newfound freedom—even if that meant driving to the same place as everyone else.

10 The Biggest Hits When You Were 10

Whistled by your father, hummed by your sister or overheard on the radio, these are the hit records as you reached double digits.

Frankie Lymon and
the Teenagers 🎵 Why Do Fools Fall in Love
Little Richard 🎵 Long Tall Sally
Fats Domino 🎵 Blueberry Hill
Carl Perkins 🎵 Blue Suede Shoes
Kay Starr 🎵 Rock and Roll Waltz
The Platters 🎵 My Prayer
The El Dorados 🎵 At My Front Door
Gene Vincent and
His Blue Caps 🎵 Be-Bop-A-Lula
Les Baxter his
Chorus and Orchestra 🎵 The Poor People of Paris
Doris Day 🎵 Que Sera, Sera
(Whatever Will Be Will Be)
Shirley and Lee 🎵 Let the Good Times Roll
Johnny Cash 🎵 I Walk the Line
Brenda Lee 🎵 Jambalaya (On the Bayou)
Ray Charles 🎵 Drown in My Own Tears
Marty Robbins 🎵 Singing the Blues
Elvis Presley 🎵 My Baby Left Me
Kitty Wells 🎵 The Lonely Side of Town
Frank Sinatra 🎵 I've Got You Under My Skin
Georgia Gibbs 🎵 I Got it Bad (and That Ain't Good)
Little Willie John 🎵 Fever
Patti Page 🎵 Allegheny Moon
Roy Orbison and Teen Kings 🎵 Ooby Dooby
Patience and Prudence 🎵 Tonight You Belong to Me
Patsy Cline 🎵 I've Loved and Lost Again

Faster, Easier, Better

Yesterday's technological breakthrough is today's modern convenience. Here are some of the lab and engineering marvels that were made before you turned 21 years old.

1946	**Waterproof diaper** The inventor of the first waterproof diaper, the Boater, was told repeatedly that no one wanted it and no one had been asking for such a thing. She decided to manufacture it herself and the product was an immediate success.
1947	Transistor
1948	Computer program
1949	Wurlitzer Select-O-Matic jukebox
1949	Zamboni ice resurfacer
1950	Teleprompter
1951	Wetsuit
1952	Artificial heart
1953	Heart-lung machine
1954	Acoustic suspension loudspeaker
1955	Pocket transistor radio
1956	Hard Disk Drive
1956	Operating system (OS)
1957	Laser
1958	Microchip
1959	Weather satellite
1960	Global navigation satellite system
1961	Spreadsheet (electronic)
1962	Red LED
1963	**Computer mouse** The inventor of the computer mouse had patented it in 1963. However, by the time the mouse became commercially available in the 1980s, his patent had expired. The first computer system that made use of a (giant) mouse came from Xerox in 1981.
1964	Plasma display
1965	Hypertext (http)
1966	Computer RAM

Across the Nation

Double digits at last: you're old enough to eavesdrop on adults and scan the headlines. These may be some of the earliest national news stories you remember.

- Eisenhower and Nixon elected to 2nd term
- "Million Dollar Quartet" meet for a recording session (Elvis, Jerry Lee Lewis, Carl Perkins, and Johnny Cash)
- Boxer Rocky Marciano retires undefeated
- IBM invents first computer hard drive
- Supreme Court declares segregated busing illegal
- Actress Grace Kelly marries royalty
- Teflon pans invented
- Video recorder (and video tape) developed
- Five missionaries killed in Ecuador
- United Methodist Church allows women to become clergy
- Two planes collide over Grand Canyon
- Dean Martin & Jerry Lewis end their partnership
- Pitcher Don Larsen throws a perfect game in World Series
- Oral vaccine for polio manufactured
- Dear Abbey answers her first letter
- First Black student to University of Alabama suspended
- In God We Trust motto authorized
- Martin Luther King Jr.'s home bombed
- Dove ice cream bar invented
- Sprinter Bobby Morrow wins 3 gold medals in 1956 Olympics
- Yahtzee goes on sale
- Robby the Robot appears
- Didrikson, voted greatest Female Athlete of the First Half of the 20th century, died
- "Does she… or doesn't she?" hair dye ad slogan coined

Born this year:
- Actress Carrie Fisher
- Actor Tom Hanks
- Illusionist David Copperfield

Kapow! Comic Books and Heroes from Your Childhood

Barely a year went past in the mid-20th Century without a new super-powered hero arriving to save the day. Here are some that were taking on the bad guys during your childhood.

Strange Adventures ✳ Captain Comet
Donald Duck ✳ Donald Duck
Uncle Scrooge ✳ Uncle Scrooge
Phantom Stranger ✳ Phantom Stranger
Wonder Woman ✳ Wonder Woman
Action Comics ✳ Superman
Detective Comics ✳ Batman
Rawhide Kid ✳ Rawhide Kid
Showcase ✳ Barry Allen
World's Finest Comics ✳ Superman
Patsy Walker ✳ Patsy Walker
Kid Colt, Outlaw ✳ Kid Colt
Mickey Mouse ✳ Mickey Mouse
Adventure Comics ✳ Aquaman
The Flash ✳ Wally West
Green Lantern ✳ Hal Jordan
Richie Rich ✳ Richie Rich
G.I. Combat ✳ The Haunted Tank
Fantastic Four ✳ The Thing

Winners of the Stanley Cup Since You Were Born

The prestigious Stanley Cup has been changing hands since 1893, although the trophy itself has been redesigned more than once. Here are the teams to lift the champagne-filled cup since you were born.

- **Detroit Red Wings (8)**
  1955: 18-year-old Larry Hillman became the youngest player to have his name engraved on the Stanley Cup trophy.

- Chicago Black Hawks (4)
- **Boston Bruins (3)**
  1970: Bobby Orr scored perhaps the most famous goal in NHL history, in midair, to clinch the title.

- **New York Rangers (1)**
  After a 1940 victory, the Rangers would not win another Stanley Cup for another 54 years.

- Toronto Maple Leafs (8)
- Montreal Canadiens (19)
- Philadelphia Flyers (2)
- New York Islanders (4)
- Edmonton Oilers (5)
- **Calgary Flames (1)**
  1989 was the last time a Stanley Cup Final has been played between two teams from Canada.

- Pittsburgh Penguins (5)
- New Jersey Devils (3)
- **Colorado Avalanche (2)**
  1996: A win in their first season after moving from Quebec (where their nickname was the Nordiques).

- Dallas Stars (1)
- Tampa Bay Lightning (3)
- Carolina Hurricanes (1)
- Anaheim Ducks (1)
- Los Angeles Kings (2)
- Washington Capitals (1)
- St. Louis Blues (1)

On the Silver Screen When You Were 11

From family favorites to the films you weren't allowed to watch, these are the films and actors that drew the praise and the crowds when you turned 11.

Gunfight at the
O.K. Corral 🎬 Burt Lancaster, Kirk Douglas, Rhonda Fleming
Island in the Sun 🎬 James Mason, Harry Belafonte, Joan Fontaine
The Prince
and the Showgirl 🎬 Marilyn Monroe, Laurence Olivier, Richard Wattis
Jailhouse Rock 🎬 Elvis Presley, Judy Tyler, Mickey Shaughnessy
Les Girls 🎬 Gene Kelly, Mitzi Gaynor, Kay Kendall
**Leslie Caron, Cyd Charisse, Jean Simmons, and Carol Haney
were considered for the female leads.**

**Et Dieu...
Créa la Femme** 🎬 Brigitte Bardot, Curd Jurgens
**The film's director and writer, Roger Vadim, was married to
its star, Brigitte Bardot. The film was heavily censored.**

Sayonara 🎬 Marlon Brando, Patricia Owens, James Garner
Peyton Place 🎬 Lana Turner, Hope Lange, Lee Philips
A Farewell to Arms 🎬 Rock Hudson, Jennifer Jones, Vittorio De Sica
The Bridge
on the River Kwai 🎬 William Holden, Jack Hawkins, Alec Guinness
The Bachelor Party 🎬 Don Murray, E.G. Marshall, Jack Warden
The Pride
and the Passion 🎬 Cary Grant, Frank Sinatra, Sophia Loren
A Face in the Crowd 🎬 Andy Griffith, Patricia Neal, Anthony Franciosa
The Incredible
Shrinking Man 🎬 Grant Williams, Randy Stuart, April Kent
Paths of Glory 🎬 Kirk Douglas, Ralph Meeker, Adolphe Menjou
Sweet Smell of Success 🎬 Burt Lancaster, Tony Curtis, Susan Harrison
12 Angry Men 🎬 Henry Fonda, Lee J. Cobb, Ed Begley
Witness for the
Prosecution 🎬 Tyrone Power, Marlene Dietrich, Charles Laughton
The Pajama Game 🎬 Doris Day, John Raitt, Carol Haney
Funny Face 🎬 Audrey Hepburn, Fred Astaire, Kay Thompson

Comic Strips You'll Know

Comic strips took off in the late 19th century and for much of the 20th century they were a dependable feature of everyday life. Some were solo efforts; others became so-called zombie strips, living on well beyond their creator. A century on, some are still going. But how many from your youth will you remember?

1940-52	The Spirit by Will Eisner
1930-	**Blondie** In 1995, Blondie was one of 20 strips commemorated by the US Postal Service in the Comic Strip Classics series.
1931-	**Dick Tracy** Gould's first idea? A detective called Plainclothes Tracy.
1930-95	Mickey Mouse
1932-	Mary Worth
1936-	**The Phantom** Lee Falk worked on The Phantom for 63 years and Mandrake The Magician for 65.
1919-	Barney Google and Snuffy Smith
1938-	Nancy
1946-	Mark Trail
1937-	**Prince Valiant** Edward, the Duke of Windsor (previously Edward VIII), called Prince Valiant the "greatest contribution to English literature in the past hundred years."
1934-2003	**Flash Gordon** Alex Raymond created Flash Gordon to compete with the Buck Rogers comic strip.
1934-77	Li'l Abner by Al Capp
1925-74	Etta Kett by Paul Robinson
1947-69	Grandma by Charles Kuhn
1948-	Rex Morgan, M.D.
1933-87	Brick Bradford
1950-2000	**Peanuts by Charles M. Schulz** Schultz was inducted into the Hockey Hall of Fame after building the Redwood Empire Arena near his studio.
1950-	Beetle Bailey

Biggest Hits by The King

He may have conquered rock'n'roll, but Elvis's success straddled genres including country music, R&B, and more. These are his Number 1s from across the charts, beginning with the rockabilly "I Forgot…" through the posthumous country hit, "Guitar Man."

I Forgot to Remember to Forget (1955)
Heartbreak Hotel (1956)
I Want You, I Need You, I Love You (1956)
Don't Be Cruel (1956)
Hound Dog (1956)
Love Me Tender (1956)
Too Much (1957)
All Shook Up (1957)
(Let Me Be Your) Teddy Bear (1957)
Jailhouse Rock (1957)
Don't (1957)
Wear My Ring Around Your Neck (1958)
Hard Headed Woman (1958)
A Big Hunk O' Love (1959)
Stuck On You (1960)
It's Now or Never (1960)
Are You Lonesome Tonight? (1960)
Surrender (1961)
Good Luck Charm (1962)
Suspicious Minds (1969)
Moody Blue (1976)
Way Down (1977)
Guitar Man (1981)

Childhood Candies

In labs across the country, mid-century food scientists dreamed up new and colorful ways to delight children just like you. These are the fruits of their labor, launched before you turned twenty-one.

1945	Dots (Mason Company)
1946	Almond Joy (Peter Paul)
1947	Bazooka Bubble Gum (Topps Candy Company)
1949	Jolly Rancher (Jolly Rancher Company)
1949	Junior Mints (James O. Welch Company)
1949	**Whoppers** (Overland Candy Company) **Whoppers were known as "Giants" before 1949.**
1949	Smarties (Ce De Candy, Inc.)
1950	Cup-O-Gold (Hoffman Candy Company)
1950	Red Vines (American Licorice Co.)
1950	Hot Tamales (Just Born)
1950	Rocky Road Candy Bar (The Annabell Candy Co.)
1952	Pixy Stix (Sunline, Inc.)
1954	Atomic Fireballs (Ferrera Candy Co.)
1954	Marshmallow Peeps (Just Born)
1954	Peanut M&Ms (Mars)
1955	**Chick-O-Sticks** (Atkinson's) **These candies were called "Chicken Bones" until they were renamed in 1955.**
1950s	Swedish Fish (Malaco)
1950s	Look! Candy Bar (Golden Nugget Candy Co.)
1960	Sixlets (Leaf Brands)
1962	Now and Later (Phoenix Candy Company)
1962	**SweeTarts** (Sunline, Inc.) **These have the same candy base as Pixy Stix which was invented using drink powder from a children's drink.**
1962	LemonHead (Ferrara Candy Company)
1963	**Cadbury Creme Eggs** (Fry's) **An original 1963 Fry's Creme Egg (as they were then called) was discovered in 2017. It hasn't been eaten.**
1964	100 Grand Bar (Nestle)
1960s	Spree (Sunline Candy Company)

Books of the Decade

Ten years of your life that took you from adventure books aged 10 to dense works of profundity at 20—or perhaps just grown-up adventures! How many did you read when they were first published?

1956	Peyton Place by Grace Metalious
1956	Giovanni's Room by James Baldwin
1956	The Return of the King by J.R.R. Tolkien
1957	On the Road by Jack Kerouac
1957	Atlas Shrugged by Ayn Rand
1958	Breakfast at Tiffany's by Truman Capote
1958	Doctor Zhivago by Boris Pasternak
1958	Exodus by Leon Uris
1959	The Haunting of Hill House by Shirley Jackson
1959	Naked Lunch by William S. Burroughs
1959	Advise and Consent by Allen Drury
1960	To Kill a Mockingbird by Harper Lee
1960	Hawaii by James Michener
1961	Catch-22 by Joseph Heller
1961	Stranger in a Strange Land by Robert A. Heinlein
1962	One Flew Over the Cuckoo's Nest by Ken Kesey
1962	Franny and Zooey by J.D. Salinger
1963	The Bell Jar by Sylvia Plath
1963	The Feminine Mystique by Betty Friedan
1963	A Clockwork Orange by Anthony Burgess
1964	The Group by Mary McCarthy
1964	Herzog by Saul Bellow
1964	The Spy Who Came in from the Cold by John le Carré
1964	Up the Down Staircase by Bel Kaufman
1965	Dune by Frank Herbert

US Buildings

Some were loathed then, loved now; others, the reverse. Some broke new architectural ground; others housed famous or infamous businesses, or helped to power a nation. All of them were built in your first 18 years.

1946	**Flamingo Hotel, Las Vegas** The Presidential Suite at The Flamingo originally featured a few extras by request of its mobster owner, "Bugsy" Siegel: bulletproof glass and a secret escape ladder. Siegel was shot dead in Beverly Hills.
1947	75 Rockefeller Plaza
1948	Mile High Stadium, Denver
1949	Promontory Apartments, Chicago
1950	Metropolitan Life North Building
1951	US General Accounting Office Building
1952	United Nations Secretariat Building
1953	Sullivan Tower, Nashville
1954	Republic Center, Dallas
1955	One Prudential Plaza, Chicago
1956	**Capitol Records Building, Los Angeles** The world's first circular office building.
1957	666 Fifth Avenue, New York City
1958	Time & Life Building, New York City
1959	2 Broadway, New York City
1960	Four Gateway Center, Pittsburgh
1961	One Chase Manhattan Plaza
1962	Kennedy Space Center, Florida
1963	**MetLife Building, New York City** The largest office space in the world when it opened, the MetLife was born as the Pan Am Building, complete with heliport and 15 ft. lit signage atop (the last permitted).
1964	277 Park Avenue, New Yor City

Radio DJs from Your Childhood

If the radio was the soundtrack to your life as you grew up, some of these voices were part of the family. (The stations listed are where these DJs made their name; the dates are their radio broadcasting career).

Wolfman Jack 🎙 XERB/Armed Forces Radio (1960–1995)
Jocko Henderson 🎙 WDAS/W LIB (1952–1991)
Casey Kasem 🎙 KRLA (1954–2010)
Kasem was the host of American Top 40 for four decades. By 1986, his show was broadcast on 1,000 radio stations.

Bruce Morrow 🎙 WABC (1959-)
Murray Kaufman 🎙 WINS (1958–1975)
You'll likely remember him as Murray the K, the self-declared "fifth Beatle" (he played a lot of music from the Fab Four).

Alison Steele 🎙 WNEW-FM (1966–1995)
Aka The Nightbird, Steele was that rarity of the sixties and seventies: a successful female DJ.

Alan Freed 🎙 WJW/WINS (1945–1965)
Freed's career crashed after he was found to have been taking payola. His contribution was recognized posthumously when admitted into the Rock n Roll Hall of Fame.

Robert W. Morgan 🎙 KHJ-AM (1955–1998)
Dan Ingram 🎙 WABC (1958–2004)
Dave Hull 🎙 KRLA (1955–2010)
Another candidate for the "fifth Beatle," Hull interviewed the band many times.

Hal Jackson 🎙 WBLS (1940–2011)
Johnny Holliday 🎙 KYA (1956-)
Herb Kent 🎙 WVON (1944–2016)
"Cool Gent" Herb Kent was the longest-serving DJ on the radio.

Tom Donahue 🎙 WIBG/KYA (1949–1975)
John R. 🎙 WLAC (1941–1973)
Bill Randle 🎙 WERE/WCBS (1940s-2004)
Jack Spector 🎙 WMCA (1955–1994)
Spector, one of WMCA's "Good Guys," died on air in 1994. A long silence after playing "I'm in the Mood for Love" alerted station staff.

It Happened in 1962

Here's a round-up of the most newsworthy events from across the US in the year you turned (sweet) 16.

- ✦ Centralia Mine catches fire (it's still burning)
- ✦ LED light demonstrated
- ✦ The Mashed Potato becomes a dance craze
- ✦ Shortest acceptance speech given for an Oscar award (Patty Duke: "Thank you.")
- ✦ With a name like Smuckers... slogan appears
- ✦ Avis rent-a-car service starts to try harder
- ✦ Cuban Missile Crisis captivates the world
- ✦ Commercial communications satellite launched
- ✦ John F. Kennedy serenaded by Marilyn Monroe on his birthday
- ✦ John Glenn orbits the Earth
- ✦ Actress Hedy Lamarr's Wifi invention implemented
- ✦ Cesar Chavez founds the United Farm Workers union
- ✦ Marilyn Monroe found dead (right)
- ✦ Taco Bell opens for business
- ✦ First video game invented (Spacewar!)
- ✦ Dr. Frances Kelsey awarded for banning thalidomide
- ✦ Wal-Mart starts selling for less
- ✦ Black student registered at University of Mississippi
- ✦ Nixon gives his "last press conference"
- ✦ Consumer Bill of Rights proposed
- ✦ Spiderman appears in comic pages
- ✦ Navy SEALs formed
- ✦ Columbus Day Storm strikes ("The Big Blow")

Born this year:
- ⚭ Actor Tom Cruise
- ⚭ Singer Jon Bon Jovi
- ⚭ Actress Jodie Foster
- ⚭ Actress Demi Moore

New York Yankees center fielder, Joe DiMaggio, was married to Marilyn Monroe in 1954; the union lasted just 9 months. But eight years later it was DiMaggio who claimed her body, kept those he blamed away from her funeral (right), and sent roses to her grave every few days for 20 years. "I'll finally get to see Marilyn," he is reported to have said shortly before he died in 1999.

News Anchors of the Fifties and Sixties

Trusted, familiar, and exclusively male: these are the faces that brought you the news, and the catchphrases they made their own.

Edward R. Murrow 📺 CBS (1938-59)
"Good night, and good luck."

Walter Cronkite 📺 CBS (1962-81)
"And that's the way it is."

David Brinkley 📺 NBC (1956-71)
"Good night, Chet..."

Chet Huntley 📺 NBC (1956-70)
"...Good night, David."

Harry Reasoner 📺 CBS & ABC (1961-91)

Frank Reynolds 📺 ABC (1968-70)

John Charles Daly 📺 CBS & ABC (1941-60)
"Good night and a good tomorrow."

Douglas Edwards 📺 CBS (1948-62)

Hugh Downs 📺 NBC (1962-71)

John Chancellor 📺 NBC (1970-82)

Paul Harvey 📺 ABC Radio (1951-2009)
"Hello Americans, this is Paul Harvey. Stand by for news!"

Mike Wallace 📺 CBS (1963-66)

John Cameron Swayze 📺 NBC (1948-56)
"Well, that's the story, folks! This is John Cameron Swayze, and I'm glad we could get together."

Ron Cochran 📺 ABC (1962-65)

Bob Young 📺 ABC (1967-68)

Dave Garroway 📺 NBC (1952-61)

Bill Shadel 📺 ABC (1960-63)

Fifties Game Shows

It all started so well: appointment radio became appointment TV, with new and crossover game shows bringing us together. But as the decade progressed, the scandal emerged: some shows were fixed. Quiz shows were down, but certainly not out. (Dates include periods off-air.)

Break the Bank 🎥 (1945–57)

Beat The Clock 🎥 (1950–2019)

Name That Tune 🎥 (1952–85)
A radio crossover that spawned 25 international versions.

Strike It Rich 🎥 (1947–58)

The Price Is Right 🎥 (1956–65)
The original version of the current quiz that began in 1972. This one was hosted by Bill Cullen.

Down You Go 🎥 (1951–56)

I've Got A Secret 🎥 (1952–2006)

What's The Story 🎥 (1951–55)

The $64,000 Question 🎥 (1955–58)

People Are Funny 🎥 (1942–60)

Tic-Tac-Dough 🎥 (1956–90)
Early Tic-Tac-Dough contestants were often coached; around three-quarters of the shows in one run were rigged.

The Name's The Same 🎥 (1951–55)

Two For The Money 🎥 (1952–57)

The Big Payoff 🎥 (1951–62)

Twenty-One 🎥 (1956–58)
At the heart of the rigging scandal, Twenty-One was the subject of Robert Redford's 1994 movie, Quiz Show.

Masquerade Party 🎥 (1952–60)

You Bet Your Life 🎥 (1947–61)
A comedy quiz hosted by Groucho Marx.

Truth or Consequences 🎥 (1940–88)
Started life as a radio quiz. TV host Bob Barker signed off with: "Hoping all your consequences are happy ones."

20 Questions 🎥 (1946–55)

What's My Line 🎥 (1950–75)

Liberty Issue Stamps

First released in 1954, the Liberty Issue drew its name from not one but three depictions of the Statue of Liberty across the denominations. (There was only room for one "real" woman, though.) It coincided with the new era of stamp collecting as a childhood hobby that endured for decades. Were you one of these new miniature philatelists?

Benjamin Franklin ½ ¢ 🖂 Polymath (writer, inventor, scientist)
Franklin discovered the principle of electricity,
the Law of Conservation of Charge.

George Washington 1 ¢ 🖂 First US President
Palace of the Governors 1 ¼ ¢ 🖂
A building in Santa Fe, New Mexico that served as
the seat of government of New Mexico for centuries.

Mount Vernon 1 ½ ¢ 🖂 George Washington's plantation
Thomas Jefferson 2 ¢ 🖂 Polymath; third US President
Bunker Hill Monument 2 ½ ¢ 🖂 Battle site of the Revolutionary War
Statue of Liberty 3 ¢ 🖂 Gifted by the people of France
Abraham Lincoln 4 ¢ 🖂 16th US President
Lincoln received a patent for a flotation device that assisted
boats in moving through shallow water.

The Hermitage 4 ½ ¢ 🖂 Andrew Jackson's plantation
James Monroe 5 ¢ 🖂 Fifth US President
Theodore Roosevelt 6 ¢ 🖂 26th US President
Woodrow Wilson 7 ¢ 🖂 28th US President; served during WW1
John J. Pershing 8 ¢ 🖂 US Army officer during World War I
Alamo 9 ¢ 🖂 Site of a pivotal Texas Revolution battle
Independence Hall 10 ¢ 🖂 Independence declared here
Benjamin Harrison 12 ¢ 🖂 23rd US President
John Jay 15 ¢ 🖂 First Chief Justice of the United States
Monticello 20 ¢ 🖂 Thomas Jefferson's plantation
Paul Revere 25 ¢ 🖂 Alerted militia of the British approach
Robert E. Lee 30 ¢ 🖂 Confederate general in the Civil War
John Marshall 40 ¢ 🖂 Fourth Chief Justice of the US
Susan B. Anthony 50 ¢ 🖂 Women's suffrage activist
Patrick Henry $1 🖂 Leader of the Dec. of Independence
Alexander Hamilton $5 🖂 First Secretary of the Treasury

The Biggest Hits When You Were 16

The artists that topped the charts when you turned 16 might not be in your top 10 these days, but you'll probably remember them!

Patsy Cline 🎸 Crazy
Ray Charles 🎸 Unchain My Heart
George Jones 🎸 She Still Thinks I Care
Pat Boone 🎸 Speedy Gonzales
Booker T. and the MGs 🎸 Green Onions
Elvis Presley 🎸 Return to Sender
Neil Sedaka 🎸 Breaking Up Is Hard to Do
Sam Cooke 🎸 Twistin' the Night Away
Bobby Vinton 🎸 Roses Are Red
Marty Robbins 🎸 Devil Woman
Joey Dee and the Starliters 🎸 Peppermint Twist
Gene Chandler 🎸 Duke of Earl
Stan Getz and Charlie Byrd 🎸 Desafinado
The Contours 🎸 Do You Love Me
Bobby "Boris" Pickett
and the Crypt Kickers 🎸 The Monster Mash
Ned Miller 🎸 From a Jack to a King
Little Eva 🎸 The Loco-Motion
Buck Owens 🎸 Save the Last Dance for Me
The Shirelles 🎸 Soldier Boy
The Four Seasons 🎸 Sherry
Tony Bennett 🎸 I Left My Heart in San Francisco
Ray Charles 🎸 You Are My Sunshine
The Miracles 🎸 You've Really Got a Hold on Me
John Lee Hooker 🎸 Boom Boom

Medical Advances Before You Were 21

A baby born in 1920 USA had a life expectancy of just 55.4 years. By 2000 that was up to 76.8, thanks to medical advances including many of these.

1946	All-glass syringe (easier sterilization)
1947	Defibrillation
1949	Intraocular lens (myopia and cataracts)
1950	**Polio vaccine** Jonas Salk was asked about taking a patent on the polio vaccine. He replied, "Can you patent the sun?"
1952	Cloning
1953	Ultrasound
1954	Kidney transplant
1955	Mass immunization of polio
1956	**Metered-dose inhaler** Invented after the teen daughter of head of Riker Labs asked why her asthma medicine couldn't be in a can like hair spray. At the time, asthma medicine was given in ineffective squeeze bulb glass containers.
1958	Pacemaker
1959	Bone marrow transplant
1959	In vitro fertilization
1960	CPR
1960	The pill
1960	Coronary artery bypass surgery
1962	Hip replacement
1962	Beta blocker
1962	First oral polio vaccine (Sabin)
1963	Liver and lung transplants
1963	Valium
1963	Artificial heart
1964	Measles vaccine
1965	Portable defibrillator
1965	Commercial ultrasound
1966	Pancreas transplant

Blockbuster Movies When You Were 16

These are the movies that everyone was talking about. How many of them did you see (or have you seen since)?

State Fair 🎟 Pat Boone, Bobby Darin, Ann-Margret

The Man Who Shot Liberty Valance 🎟 John Wayne, James Stewart, Lee Marvin

Bon Voyage! 🎟 Fred MacMurray, Jane Wyman, Deborah Walley

Gypsy 🎟 Karl Malden, Rosalind Russell, Natalie Wood

Hatari! 🎟 John Wayne, Hardy Kruger, Elsa Martinelli

Lolita 🎟 James Mason, Shelley Winters, Peter Sellers

That Touch of Mink 🎟 Cary Grant, Doris Day, Gig Young

Cary Grant reportedly asked Citroen for a new roadster to use in the film. A new model Citroen DS 19 was promptly dispatched to him.

The Music Man 🎟 Robert Preston, Shirley Jones, Buddy Hackett

The Interns 🎟 Michael Callan, Cliff Robertson, James MacArthur

Kid Galahad 🎟 Elvis Presley, Lola Albright, Gig Young

The Longest Day 🎟 John Wayne, Henry Fonda, Robert Mitchum

The Manchurian Candidate 🎟 Frank Sinatra, Laurence Harvey, Janet Leigh

Mutiny on The Bounty 🎟 Marlon Brando, Trevor Howard, Richard Harris

Girls! Girls! Girls! 🎟 Elvis Presley, Stella Stevens, Laurel Goodwin

Lawrence of Arabia 🎟 Alec Guinness, Anthony Quinn, Jack Hawkins

Taras Bulba 🎟 Yul Brynner, Tony Curtis, Perry Lopez

In Search of the Castaways 🎟 Hayley Mills, Maurice Chevalier, George Sanders

To Kill A Mockingbird 🎟 Gregory Peck, Mary Badham, Phillip Alford

Days of Wine and Roses 🎟 Jack Lemmon, Lee Remick, Charles Bickford

What Ever Happened to Baby Jane? 🎟 Betty Davis, Joan Crawford, Victor Buono

The Miracle Worker 🎟 Anne Bancroft, Patty Duke, Victor Jory

Long Day's Journey into Night 🎟 Katharine Hepburn, Ralph Richardson

How the West Was Won 🎟 Carroll Baker, Walter Brennan, Lee J. Cobb

Game Show Hosts of the Fifties and Sixties

Many of these men were semi-permanent fixtures, their voices and catchphrases ringing through the decades. Some were full-time entertainers; others were on sabbatical from more serious news duties.

John Charles Daly ➤ What's My Line (1950–67)

Art Linkletter ➤ People Are Funny (1943–60)

Garry Moore ➤ I've Got A Secret (1956–64)

Groucho Marx ➤ You Bet Your Life (1949–61)

Warren Hull ➤ Strike It Rich (1947–58)

Herb Shriner ➤ Two For The Money (1952–56)

George DeWitt ➤ Name That Tune (1953–59)

Robert Q. Lewis ➤ Name's The Same (1951–54)

Bill Cullen ➤ The Price Is Right (1956–65)

Walter Cronkite ➤ It's News To Me (1954)
"The most trusted man in America" was briefly the host of this topical quiz game. He didn't do it again.

Bill Slater ➤ 20 Questions (1949–52)

Walter Kiernan ➤ Who Said That (1951–54)

Bob Eubanks ➤ The Newlywed Game (1966–74)

Bud Collyer ➤ To Tell The Truth (1956–69)

Jack Barry ➤ Twenty-One (1956–58)

Bert Parks ➤ Break The Bank (1945–57)

Hugh Downs ➤ Concentration (1958–69)

Mike Stokey ➤ Pantomime Quiz (1947–59)

Allen Ludden ➤ Password (1961–75)

Bob Barker ➤ Truth or Consequences (1956–74)
Barker also spent 35 years hosting **The Price Is Right**.

Hal March ➤ $64,000 Question (1955–58)

Monty Hall ➤ Let's Make A Deal (1963–91)
Monty—born "Monte", but misspelled on an early publicity photo—was also a philanthropist who raised around $1 billion over his lifetime.

Johnny Carson ➤ Who Do You Trust? (1957–63)

Kitchen Inventions

The 20th-century kitchen was a playground for food scientists and engineers with new labor-saving devices and culinary shortcuts launched every year. These all made their debut before you were 18.

1946	Food processor
1946	Tupperware products
1947	Zen Rex speed peeler
1948	Aluminum foil
1949	**Reddi-Wip cream**

Reddi-Wip has been chosen as one of The Top 100 consumer inventions of 20th century and made its inventor, Aaron Lapin, the 'Whipped Cream King', millions of dollars.

1950	Green Garbage Bags
1951	Kenwood food mixer
1952	Automatic coffee pot
1952	Bread clip
1953	Combination washer-dryer
1954	Zipper storage bag
1955	Lint roller
1956	Saran wrap
1957	Homemaker tableware
1958	Rice-a-Roni
1959	Chocolate Velvet Cake invented
1960	**Automated dishwasher**

Electric dishwashers debuted in 1929 but to little acclaim, due in part to the Great Depression and WWII. Automated models with a drying element finally became popular in the 1970s.

1961	Mrs. Butterworth's syrup
1962	Chimney starter
1963	**Veg-O-Matic**

The Veg-O-Matic has increased the cultural lexicon in a number of ways, including "As Seen On TV" and "It slices and dices."

Around the World When You Turned 18

These are the headlines from around the globe as you were catapulted into adulthood.

- Shinkansen (bullet train) begins running
- Malta gains independence
- Plans are made for tunnel under the English Channel
- South Africa banned from Olympics
- PLO is established
- UK sentences Great Train Robbers to 30 years
- Little Mermaid head is stolen
- Olympics open in Tokyo
- Berlin tunnel escape
- Austria hosts the Winter Olympics
- Woman flies around globe
- China tests the atomic bomb
- Tanzania is formed
- Revolution begins in Zanzibar
- Anti-Muslim riots take place in Calcutta
- Mandela is jailed
- Italy seeks help in keeping Tower of Pisa from falling over
- King steps down in Saudi Arabia
- Massacre at school in West Germany
- Civil war begins in Cyprus
- Soccer match disaster in Peru kills over 300, the world's worst
- Coup overthrows government in Brazil
- South Korea declares martial law

Super Bowl Champions Since You Were Born

These are the teams that have held a 7-pound, sterling silver Vince Lombardi trophy aloft during the Super Bowl era, and the number of times they've done it in your lifetime.

- **New England Patriots (6)**
  2001: The Super Bowl MVP, Tom Brady, had been a 6th round draft pick in 2000.
- Pittsburgh Steelers (6)
- Dallas Cowboys (5)
- San Francisco 49ers (5)
- **Green Bay Packers (4)**
  1967: To gain a berth in the Super Bowl, the Packers defeated the Dallas Cowboys in The Ice Bowl at 15 degrees below zero.
- New York Giants (4)
- **Denver Broncos (3)**
  2015: After the Broncos won their first Super Bowl 18 years prior, Broncos owner Pat Bowlen dedicated the victory to long-time quarterback John Elway ("This one's for John!"). After the 2015 victory, John Elway (now general manager) dedicated it to the ailing Bowlen ("This one's for Pat!").
- Washington Football Team (3)
- Las Vegas Raiders (3)
- Miami Dolphins (2)
- Indianapolis Colts (2)
- Kansas City Chiefs (2)
- Baltimore Ravens (2)
- Tampa Bay Buccaneers (2)
- **St. Louis/Los Angeles Rams (2)**
  1999: The Rams were led to the Super Bowl by Kurt Warner, who had been a grocery store clerk after college.
- Seattle Seahawks (1)
- Philadelphia Eagles (1)
- **Chicago Bears (1)**
  The 1985 Bears are known for their song, The Super Bowl Shuffle.
- New York Jets (1)
- New Orleans Saints (1)

Across the Nation

18

Voting. Joining the military. Turning 18 is serious stuff. Here's what everyone was reading about in the year you reached this milestone.

- Martin Luther King Jr. selected Time's Man of the Year
- State lottery in New Hampshire begins
- G.I. Joe action figure bursts onto the scene
- Twenty-Fourth amendment ratified
- Rock'em Sock'em Robots introduced
- Pepsi Cola coins "the Pepsi generation"
- Mr. Whipple tells people to stop squeezing the Charmin
- Boston Strangler captured
- Ronald Reagan makes "A Time For Choosing" speech
- Civil Rights Act of 1964 passed
- World's Fair held in New York City
- Lyndon Johnson elected for president
- Sharpie marker introduced
- Malcolm X meets Martin Luther King Jr. (right)
- First political attack ad, "Daisy Girl," broadcast
- President Johnson declares "War on Poverty"
- Astronaut John Glenn runs for Senate
- Daisy Girl's target—Senator Barry Goldwater—runs for president
- Good Friday Earthquake strikes Alaska
- Draft cards are burned in protest
- Mississippi Burning: civil rights workers murdered
- Race riot on the streets of Philadelphia
- Warren Commission Report published
- Martin Luther King Jr. awarded Nobel Peace Prize

Born this year:
- Vice President Kamala Harris
- First Lady Michelle Obama
- Amazon founder Jeff Bezos
- Actress Courtney Cox

Mary Evans Picture Library

The only meeting between Martin Luther King and Malcolm X was a fleeting and unplanned encounter on Capitol Hill. Both were attending a hearing on a bill proposed by JFK—and now taken on by Lyndon Johnson—to end segregation. The differing approaches of these civil rights activists had kept them apart; Malcolm X had previously declined an invitation to meet. And although Malcolm X was in the crowd as King declared "I have a dream" at the 1963 March on Washington, to Malcom X the event had been a circus and a farce.

But in 1964, a meeting of minds seemed possible. Malcolm X had split from The Nation of Islam and told King that he was throwing himself "into the heart of the civil rights struggle." In 1965, while King was in jail, Malcolm X met Coretta Scott King and explained that he was there to encourage protesters to listen to her husband by showing "White people ... what the alternative was."

US Open Champions

Winners while you were between the ages of the youngest (John McDermott, 1911, 19 years) and the oldest (Hale Irwin,1990, at 45). Planning a win? Better hurry up!

1965	**Gary Player** First non-US winner of the US Open since 1925.
1966	Billy Casper
1967	Jack Nicklaus
1968	Lee Trevino
1969	Orville Moody
1970	Tony Jacklin
1971	Lee Trevino
1972	Jack Nicklaus
1973	**Johnny Miller** In 1973, 61-year-old Sam Snead became the oldest player ever to make the cut.
1974	Hale Irwin
1975	Lou Graham
1976	Jerry Pate
1977	Hubert Green
1978	Andy North
1979	Hale Irwin
1980	**Jack Nicklaus** Nicklaus set the record for years (18) between the first and last US Open victory.
1981	David Graham
1982	Tom Watson
1983	Larry Nelson
1984	Fuzzy Zoeller
1985	Andy North
1986	Raymond Floyd
1987	Scott Simpson
1988	Curtis Strange
1989	Curtis Strange
1990	Hale Irwin
1991	Payne Stewart

Popular Girls' Names

If you started a family at a young age, these are the names you're most likely to have chosen. And even if you didn't pick them, a lot of Americans did!

Lisa

Lisa's fifth year in the top spot, having toppled Mary. Lisa would stay there until 1969 (when she was usurped by Jennifer).

Kimberly
Mary
Michelle
Karen
Susan
Patricia
Tammy
Angela
Jennifer
Cynthia
Donna
Julie
Pamela
Deborah
Elizabeth
Sandra
Linda
Laura
Christine
Lori
Melissa
Tina
Dawn
Brenda
Kelly

Rising and falling stars:

Heidi, Stacy, Tonya, Tamara and Holly graced the Top 100 for the first time; for Bonnie, Darlene, Judy and Cathy it would be their last ever year in the spotlight.

Animals Extinct in Your Lifetime

Billions of passenger pigeons once flew the US skies. By 1914, they had been trapped to extinction. Not every species dies at our hands, but it's a sobering roll-call. (Date is year last known alive or declared extinct).

1949	Sinu parakeet
1951	Yemen gazelle
1952	**Deepwater cisco fish**

The deepwater cisco, once found in Lake Huron and Michigan, was overfished and crowded out by invasive parasites and alewife herring. Result? Extinction.

1952	San Benedicto rock wren
1960	Candango mouse, Brasilia
1962	Red-bellied opossum, Argentina
1963	Kākāwahie honeycreeper, Hawaii
1964	South Island snipe, New Zealand
1966	Arabian ostrich
1967	Saint Helena earwig
1967	**Yellow blossom pearly mussel**

Habitat loss and pollution proved terminal for this Tennessee resident.

1971	Lake Pedder earthworm, Tasmania
1972	Bushwren, New Zealand
1977	Siamese flat-barbelled catfish, Thailand
1981	Southern gastric-brooding frog, Australia
1986	Las Vegas dace
1989	Golden toad (see right)
1990	Dusky seaside sparrow, East Coast USA
2000	**Pyrenean ibex, Iberia**

For a few minutes in 2003 this species was brought back to life through cloning, but sadly the newborn female ibex died.

2001	Caspian tiger, Central Asia
2008	Saudi gazelle
2012	**Pinta giant tortoise**

The rarest creature in the world for the latter half of his 100-year life, Lonesome George of the Galapagos was the last remaining Pinta tortoise.

The observed history of the golden toad is brief and tragic. It wasn't discovered until 1964, abundant in a pristine area of Costa Rica. By 1989 it had gone, a victim of rising temperatures.

Popular Boys' Names

Here are the top boys' names for this year. Many of the most popular choices haven't shifted much since you were born, but more modern names are creeping in…

Michael
For 44 years from 1954 onwards, Michael was the nation's most popular name. (There was one blip in 1960 when David came first.)

David
James
John
Robert
William
Mark
Richard
Jeffrey
Thomas
Timothy
Christopher
Steven
Brian
Joseph
Scott
Kevin
Paul
Daniel
Charles
Kenneth
Anthony
Gregory
Ronald
Eric
Stephen
Donald

Rising and falling stars:
Just one year after his 68th placing, Darryl was heading for the door in 1966, along with Harold. Jason and Tracy made their first appearances.

Popular Movies When You Were 21

The biggest stars in the biggest movies: these are the films the nation were enjoying as you entered into adulthood.

El Dorado 🎬 John Wayne, Robert Mitchum, James Caan

The Jungle Book 🎬 Phil Harris, Sebastian Cabot, George Sanders
The Beatles were planned to appear, but John Lennon refused to work on animated films.

In the Heat of the Night 🎬 Sidney Poitier, Rod Steiger, Lee Grant

Valley of the Dolls 🎬 Barbara Parkins, Patty Duke, Sharon Tate

In Like Flint 🎬 James Coburn, Lee J. Cobb, Jerry Goldsmith

Divorce American Style 🎬 Dick Van Dyke, Debbie Reynolds, Jason Robards

Guess Who's Coming to Dinner 🎬 Spencer Tracy, Sidney Poitier, Katharine Hepburn

The Born Losers 🎬 Tom Laughlin, Elizabeth James, Jeremy Slate

Doctor Dolittle 🎬 Rex Harrison, Samantha Eggar, Anthony Newley

Dirty Dozen 🎬 Lee Marvin, Ernest Borgnine, Jim Brown

The Graduate 🎬 Dustin Hoffman, Anne Bancroft, Katharine Ross

The War Wagon 🎬 John Wayne, Kirk Douglas, Howard Keel

The Taming of the Shrew 🎬 Elizabeth Taylor, Richard Burton, Natasha Pyne

In Cold Blood 🎬 Robert Blake, Scott Wilson, John Forsythe

Hombre 🎬 Paul Newman, Frederic March, Richard Boone

Thoroughly Modern Millie 🎬 Julie Andrews, Mary Tyler Moore, James Fox

Wait Until Dark 🎬 Audrey Hepburn, Alan Arkin, Richard Crenna

Casino Royale 🎬 Peter Sellers, Ursula Andress, Barbara Bouchet

Camelot 🎬 Richard Harris, Vanessa Redgrave, Franco Nero

The Ambushers 🎬 Dean Martin, Senta Berger, Janice Rule

Cool Hand Luke 🎬 Paul Newman, George Kennedy, J.D. Cannon

Bonnie and Clyde 🎬 Warren Beatty, Faye Dunaway

To Sir With Love 🎬 Sidney Poitier, Christian Roberts, Judy Geeson
The film's title song was the best-selling single in the United States in 1967.

You Only Live Twice 🎬 Sean Connery, Akiko Wakabayashi, Mie Hama

Across the Nation

A selection of national headlines from the year you turned 21. But how many can you remember?

- ✦ Thurgood Marshall sworn into the Supreme Court
- ✦ Stalin's daughter defects to US
- ✦ Battleship (the game) sets sail
- ✦ Maytag repairman becomes the loneliest guy
- ✦ Handheld calculator invented
- ✦ 7-11 Slurpees offered nationwide
- ✦ Green Bay Packers win Super Bowl
- ✦ Saint Louis Cardinals win World Series
- ✦ Astronauts die in Apollo launchpad fire
- ✦ Twenty-Fifth Amendment ratified
- ✦ Human Be-in begins the "Summer of Love"
- ✦ Muhammad Ali refuses military service
- ✦ Martin Luther King Jr. speaks out against the Vietnam War
- ✦ Tornadoes strike Midwest
- ✦ Supreme Court decides Loving v. Virginia
- ✦ Freedom of Information Act goes into effect
- ✦ Riots in Detroit and other cities increase (right)
- ✦ Future senator John McCain shot down as a navy pilot
- ✦ Vietnam protest march on the Pentagon
- ✦ Apollo 4 test spacecraft launched
- ✦ Big Mac introduced locally, then nationally
- ✦ Corporation for Public Broadcasting founded
- ✦ National Transportation Safety Board (NTSB) created
- ✦ JFK's eternal flame lit at Arlington National Cemetery

Born this year:
- ☙ Actor Matt LeBlanc
- ☙ Actress Julia Roberts
- ☙ Talk show host Jimmy Kimmel

July 1967: of the many race riots over the course of that summer, few were as intense or long-lived as the disturbances in Detroit. For five days, fires were set and stores looted. The National Guard and US Army Airborne divisions were called in to quell the violence; 43 died, and damage ran to tens of millions of dollars

The Biggest Hits When You Were 21

The artists you love at 21 are with you for life. How many of these hits from this milestone year can you still hum or sing in the tub?

Frankie Valli ♪ Can't Take My Eyes Off
Loretta Lynn ♪ Don't Come Home A' Drinkin'
(With Lovin' on Your Mind)
Procol Harum ♪ A White Shade of Pale
The Box Tops ♪ The Letter
The Turtles ♪ Happy Together
Aretha Franklin ♪ Respect
The Rolling Stones ♪ Let's Spend
the Night Together
Glen Campbell ♪ Gentle on My Mind
Johnny Cash and June Carter ♪ Jackson
Sam & Dave ♪ Soul Man
Diana Ross and the Supremes ♪ Reflections
The Spencer Davis Group ♪ Gimme Some Lovin'
Tammy Wynette ♪ I Don't Want to Play House
The Who ♪ I Can See for Miles
Van Morrison ♪ Brown Eyed Girl
Jimi Hendrix ♪ Hey Joe
The Young Rascals ♪ Groovin'
Stevie Wonder ♪ I Was Made to Love Her
Sonny and Cher ♪ And the Beat Goes On
Marvin Gaye and Tammi Terrell ♪ Ain't No Mountain
High Enough
Aaron Neville ♪ Tell It Like It Is
Dionne Warwick ♪ I Say a Little Prayer
The Beatles ♪ All You Need Is Love
The Doors ♪ Light My Fire

Popular Food in the 1960s

Changes in society didn't stop at the front door: a revolution in the kitchen brought us exotic new recipes, convenience in a can, and even space-age fruit flavors. These are the tastes of a decade, but how many of them were on the menu for your family?

McDonald's Big Mac
First served in 1967 by a Pittsburgh franchisee.
Royal Shake-a-Pudd'n Dessert Mix
Tunnel of Fudge Cake
Campbell's SpaghettiOs
Pop-Tarts
B&M's canned bread
Cool Whip
A time-saving delight that originally contained no milk or cream, meaning that it could be frozen and transported easily.

Grasshopper pie
Beech-Nut Fruit Stripe Gum
Sandwich Loaf
Lipton Onion Soup Dip
Millions of packets are still sold each year of this favorite that was once known as "Californian Dip".

Jello salad
Hires Root Beer
Baked Alaska
Tang
Invented by William A. Mitchell who also concocted Cool Whip, Tang was used by astronauts to flavor the otherwise unpalatable water on board the Gemini and Apollo missions.

Corn Diggers
Teem soda
Eggo Waffles
Kraft Shake 'N Bake
Maypo oatmeal
In 1985, Dire Straights sang, "I want my MTV"—an echo of the stars who'd shouted the same words to promote the new station. But 30 years before that (and the inspiration for MTV's campaign), an animated child yelled, "I want my Maypo!"

Fashion in the Sixties

As a child, you (generally) wear what you're given. It's only in hindsight, on fading Polaroids, that you recognize that your outfits carried the fashion imprint of the day. Whether you were old or bold enough to carry off a pair of bell bottoms, though, is a secret that should remain between you and your photo albums.

Bell bottoms
Bell bottoms were widely available at Navy surplus and thrift stores at a time when second-hand shopping was on the rise.

Miniskirts and mini dresses

Peasant blouses

Rudi Gernreich
Pope Paul IV banned Catholics from wearing his monokini—a topless swim suit.

US flag clothing

Tulle turbans

Shift dresses

Collarless jackets
This jacket trend was popularized by the Beatles in 1963.

Babydoll dresses

V-neck tennis sweaters

Afghan coats

Leopard print clothing
In 1962, Jackie Kennedy wore a leopard print coat which caused a spike in demand for leopard skin, leading to the death of up to 250,000 leopards. The coat's designer, Oleg Cassini, felt guilty about it for the rest of his life.

Tie-dye clothing

Short, brightly colored, shapeless dresses

Pillbox hats

Mary Quant

Maxi skirts

Bonnie Cashin

Plaid

Poor boy sweaters

Pea coats

Around the World When You Turned 25

With the growing reach of news organizations, events from outside our borders were sometimes front-page news. How many do you remember?

✦ British troops sent to Ireland
✦ India clashes with Pakistan
✦ Qatar gains independence
✦ Soviets launch space station
✦ United Arab Emirates is established
✦ Bangladesh created
✦ UN admits China as member
✦ Stairway collapse kills 66 in Scottish stadium
✦ Peru hit by earthquake
✦ Idi Amin comes to power in Uganda
✦ Mount Etna erupts
✦ Turkish earthquakes devastate the country
✦ IRA sets off bomb in London post office
✦ Switzerland grants women the right to vote
✦ Sierra Leone becomes independent
✦ Japan launches world's largest supertanker
✦ Accident on Soyuz 11 kills 3 cosmonauts
✦ Montreal receives over 16 feet of snow in one storm
✦ Coup overthrows government in Bolivia
✦ Australia and New Zealand withdraw troops from Vietnam
✦ Cyclone off Indian coast kills thousands
✦ Largest hydroelectric plant opens in Soviet Union
✦ French doctors found Doctors Without Borders
✦ Bulanti motorcar is built in Australia
✦ Cambodia is rocked by civil war

Cars of the 1960s

Smaller cars. More powerful cars. More distinctive cars. More variety, yes: but the success of imported models such as the Volkswagen Beetle was a sign that more fundamental changes lay ahead for The Big Three.

1940	Ford Lincoln Continental
1949	Volkswagen Beetle
1950	Volkswagen Type 2 (Microbus)
1958	**General Motors Chevrolet Impala**
	In 1965, the Impala sold more than 1 million units, the most sold by any model in the US since WWII.
1958	American Motors Corporation Rambler Ambassador
1959	General Motors Chevrolet El Camino
1959	Ford Galaxie
1960	**Ford Falcon**
	The cartoon strip "Peanuts" was animated for TV to market the Falcon.
1960	General Motors Pontiac Tempest
1960	General Motors Chevrolet Corvair
1961	**Jaguar E-Type**
	Ranked first in The Daily Telegraph UK's list of the world's "100 most beautiful cars" of all time.
1961	Chrysler Newport
1962	Shelby Cobra
1963	General Motors Buick Riviera
1963	Porsche 911
1963	Kaiser-Jeep Jeep Wagoneer
1964	**Ford Mustang**
	The song of the same name reached #6 on the R&B Charts in 1966. That year, more Ford Mustangs were sold (550,000) than any other car.
1964	General Motors Chevrolet Chevelle
1964	Chrysler Plymouth Barracuda
1964	General Motors Pontiac GTO
1967	General Motors Chevrolet Camaro
1967	Ford Mercury Cougar
1968	Chrysler Plymouth Road Runner

Books of the Decade

Were you a voracious bookworm in your twenties? Or a more reluctant reader, only drawn by the biggest titles of the day? Here are the new titles that fought for your attention.

1966	Valley of the Dolls by Jacqueline Susann
1966	In Cold Blood by Truman Capote
1967	Rosemary's Baby by Ira Levin
1967	The Arrangement by Elia Kazan
1967	The Confessions of Nat Turner by William Styron
1968	Airport by Arthur Hailey
1968	Couples by John Updike
1969	The Godfather by Mario Puzo
1969	Slaughterhouse-Five by Kurt Vonnegut
1969	Portnoy's Complaint by Philip Roth
1969	The French Lieutenant's Woman by John Fowles
1970	Love Story by Erich Segal
1970	One Hundred Years of Solitude by Gabriel Garcia Marquez
1971	The Happy Hooker: My Own Story by Xaviera Hollander
1971	The Exorcist by William Peter Blatty
1972	Watership Down by Richard Adams
1972	The Joy of Sex by Alex Comfort
1972	Fear and Loathing in Las Vegas by Hunter S. Thompson
1973	Fear of Flying by Erica Jong
1973	Gravity's Rainbow by Thomas Pynchon
1974	Jaws by Peter Benchley
1974	The Front Runner by Patricia Nell Warren
1975	The Eagle Has Landed by Jack Higgins
1975	Shōgun by James Clavell
1975	Ragtime by E.L. Doctorow

Prominent Americans

This new set of definitive stamps, issued from 1965 onwards, aimed to do a better job of capturing the diversity of the Americans who made a nation. The series doubled the previous number of women depicted...to two. How many did you have in your collection?

Thomas Jefferson 1 ¢ Third US President
Albert Gallatin 1 ¼ ¢ Fourth Treasury Secretary
Frank Lloyd Wright 2 ¢ Architect
Francis Parkman 3 ¢ Historian
Abraham Lincoln 4 ¢ 16th US President
George Washington 5 ¢ First US President
Franklin D Roosevelt 6 ¢ 32nd US President
Dwight Eisenhower 6 / 8 ¢ 34th US President
In 1957, Eisenhower became the first president to travel by helicopter instead of a limo, en route to Camp David (which he had called Shangri-La, but renamed after his grandson).

Benjamin Franklin 7 ¢ Polymath
Albert Einstein 8 ¢ Physicist
Andrew Jackson 10 ¢ 7th US President
Henry Ford 12 ¢ Founder of Ford Motor Company
John F. Kennedy 13 ¢ 35th US President
Fiorello LaGuardia 14 ¢ Mayor of New York City in WWII
Read Dick Tracy comics on the radio during a paper strike.

Oliver Wendell Holmes, Jr 15 ¢ Supreme Court Justice
Ernie Pyle 16 ¢ Journalist during World War II
Elizabeth Blackwell 18 ¢ First woman to get a medical degree.
After 11 college rejections, male students at Geneva Medical College all voted for her acceptance. They did it as a joke.

George C Marshall 20 ¢ Sec. of State and Sec. of Defense
Amadeo Giannini 21 ¢ Founder of Bank of America
Frederick Douglass 25 ¢ Slavery escapee, abolitionist leader
John Dewey 30 ¢ Educational pioneer
Thomas Paine 40 ¢ Helped inspire the American Revolution
Lucy Stone 50 ¢ Suffragist and slavery campaigner
Eugene O'Neill $1 Playwright
John Bassett Moore $5 Jurist

Sixties Game Shows

Recovery from the quiz show scandal of the fifties was a gradual process. Big prize money was out; games were in—the sillier the better, or centered around relationships. "Popcorn for the mind," as game show creator Chuck Barris memorably put it.

College Bowl 🏆 (1953-70)
Snap Judgment 🏆 (1967-69)
To Tell The Truth 🏆 (1956-present)
Dough Re Mi 🏆 (1958-60)
Camouflage 🏆 (1961-62 & 1980)
Dream House 🏆 (1968-84)
Say When!! 🏆 (1961-65)
Let's Make A Deal 🏆 (1963-present)
The long-time presenter of the show, Monty Hall, gave rise to the eponymous problem: when one door in three hides a prize and you've made your pick, should you change your answer when the host reveals a "zonk" (dud) behind another door? (The counterintuitive answer is yes!)

Your First Impression 🏆 (1962-64)
Supermarket Sweep 🏆 (1965-present)
In one of its many comebacks, 1990 episodes of Supermarket Sweep featured monsters roaming the aisles including Frankenstein and Mr. Yuk.

You Don't Say! 🏆 1963-79)
It's Your Bet 🏆 (1969-73)
Yours For A Song 🏆 (1961-63)
Concentration 🏆 (1958-91)
Seven Keys 🏆 (1960-65)
Queen For A Day 🏆 1945-1970)
Password 🏆 (1961-75)
Video Village 🏆 (1960-62)
Who Do You Trust? 🏆 (1957-63)
Originally titled, "Do You Trust Your Wife?"
Personality 🏆 (1967-69)
Beat The Odds 🏆 (1961-69)

Across the Nation

Another decade passes and you're well into adulthood. Were you reading the news, or making it? Here are the national stories that dominated the front pages.

- Bicentennial celebrations around the country
- Apple computers founded
- Quarters released with "1776–1976"
- US Mint releases $2 bill
- Viking I lands on Mars
- Last slide rule manufactured
- Cray-1 Supercomputer installed
- FDA bans Red Dye #2
- Commercial laser printer available
- Hair Club for Men founded
- Jimmy Carter elected president (right)
- Space shuttle launches
- 34 die after American Legion convention; bacteria is named Legionella
- New York City terrorized by "Son of Sam" killer
- Gunmen kidnap school bus full of children
- US men dominate swimming in 1976 Olympics
- George Washington promoted to 6-star general
- Consecutive Super Bowl win for Pittsburgh Steelers
- Cincinnati Reds win another World Series
- Black History Month begins
- 1970s declared the "Me" decade
- Perrier bottled water goes on sale
- Natalie Cole receives Grammy for Best New Artist
- Hank Aaron hits his last (775th) home run

Born this year:
- Actor Chadwick Boseman
- Actress Alicia Silverstone
- Twitter cofounder Jack Dorsey

Keystone Press Agency/Keystone USA via ZUMAPRESS.com/Mary Evans

"Jimmy Who is Running for What!?" a newspaper in Jimmy Carter's home state of Georgia asked after he announced his intention to run for president. But in 1976, an effective national strategy, his status as an "outsider," and favorable media coverage took the former peanut farmer and nuclear physicist all the way to the White House.

The Biggest Hits When You Were 30...

How many of these big tunes from the year you turned thirty will still strike a chord decades later?

Paul McCartney and Wings ♪ Let 'Em In
Elton John and Kiki Dee ♪ Don't Go Breaking My Heart
The Four Seasons ♪ December 1963
(Oh, What a Night)
Rod Stewart ♪ Tonight's the Night
Wild Cherry ♪ Play That Funky Music
Walter Murphy
and the Big Apple Band ♪ A Fifth of Beethoven
Starland Vocal Band ♪ Afternoon Delight
Gary Wright ♪ Dream Weaver
Manfred Mann's Earth Band ♪ Blinded by the Light
The Eagles ♪ Take It to the Limit
Earth, Wind and Fire ♪ Sing a Song
Chicago ♪ If You Leave Me Now
Leo Sayer ♪ You Make Me Feel Like Dancing
Steve Miller Band ♪ Rock'n Me
Stevie Wonder ♪ I Wish
Diana Ross ♪ Love Hangover
Boston ♪ More Than a Feeling
Engelbert Humperdinck ♪ After the Lovin'
Waylon Jennings
and Willie Nelson ♪ Good Hearted Woman
Daryl Hall and John Oates ♪ She's Gone
Abba ♪ Dancing Queen
The Manhattans ♪ Kiss and Say Goodbye
Queen ♪ Bohemian Rhapsody
The Bellamy Brothers ♪ Let Your Love Flow

...and the Movies You Saw That Year, Too

From award winners to crowd pleasers, here are the movies that played as your third decade drew to a close.

The Bad News Bears 🎞 Walter Matthau, Tatum O'Neal, Vic Morrow

Midway 🎞 Charlton Heston, Henry Fonda, James Coburn

Taxi Driver 🎞 Robert De Niro, Jodie Foster, Cybill Shepherd

Mother, Jugs & Speed 🎞 Bill Cosby, Raquel Welch, Harvey Keitel

Murder by Death 🎞 Eileen Brennan, Truman Capote, James Coco

Silent Movie 🎞 Mel Brooks, Marty Feldman, Dom DeLuise

Gator 🎞 Burt Reynolds, Jack Weston, Lauren Hutton

Logan's Run 🎞 Michael York, Jenny Agutter, Richard Jordan

The Omen 🎞 Gregory Peck, Lee Remick, David Warner

King Kong 🎞 Jeff Bridges, Charles Grodin, Jessica Lange

The Outlaw Josey Wales 🎞 Clint Eastwood, Chief Dan George

Rocky 🎞 Sylvester Stallone, Talia Shire, Burt Young
Stallone reportedly wrote the screenplay of Rocky in 3½ days.

The Enforcer 🎞 Clint Eastwood, Tyne Daly, DeVeren Bookwalter

A Star is Born 🎞 Barbra Streisand, Kris Kristofferson, Gary Busey

Marathon Man 🎞 Dustin Hoffman, Laurence Olivier, Roy Scheider

All the President's Men 🎞 Robert Redford, Dustin Hoffman

Carrie 🎞 Sissy Spacek, John Travolta, Piper Laurie

The Pink Panther Strikes Again 🎞 Peter Sellers, Herbert Lom, Lesley-Anne Down

To Fly! 🎞 Ellen Bry, Jennifer Kaye Evans

Silver Streak 🎞 Gene Wilder, Richard Pryor, Jill Clayburgh

In Search of Noah's Ark 🎞 Brad Crandall, Vern Adix

Network 🎞 Faye Dunaway, William Holden, Peter Finch
Beatrice Straight occupied only 5:02 of screen time, making it the shortest performance to ever win an Oscar.

The Pom Pom Girls 🎞 Robert Carradine, Jennifer Ashley, Michael Mullins

Around the House

Sometimes with a fanfare but often by stealth, inventions and innovations transformed the 20th-century household. Here's what arrived between the ages of 10 and 30.

1956	Snooze alarm clock
1956	Velcro
1957	Off mosquito repellent
1957	First electric watch
1958	Friskies cat food
1959	Princess line telephone
1961	Head & Shoulders shampoo
1963	**Chips Ahoy! chocolate chip cookies**

An elementary teacher and her class wrote Nabisco saying that they did not find 1000 chips in the bag of Chips Ahoy, though the bag clearly states it has that many. Nabisco flew a representative to their school and demonstrated to the students (and the media) how to actually find all the chips.

1963	Push button Touchtone phone
1963	Lava lamps
1964	Portable TVs
1964	Sharpie permanent markers
1965	Cordless telephone
1967	Close-up toothpaste
1968	Bean bag chair
1970	**Irish Spring soap**

Irish Spring soap's catchy tune and tag lines became part of the language with "Clean as a whistle" and "I like it too!" While it generated a lot of bad Irish accents, it has nothing to do with Ireland.

1971	Soft contact lenses
1972	Science calculator
1973	BIC lighter
1974	Rubik's Cube
1975	Betamax video tape machine

Here's one that didn't quite make the grade: AT&T's Picturephone, demonstrated here at the 1964 New York World's Fair. A trial set up that year invited the public to rent two of the Picturephone rooms set up in New York, Chicago, and Washington ($16 for 3 minutes). The take-up over the following years was almost nil, but Picturephones went on sale in 1970 anyway with a prediction of a billion-dollar business by 1980. The devices were withdrawn from sale in 1973.

Female Olympic Gold Medalists in Your Lifetime

These are the women who have stood atop the podium the greatest number of times at the Summer Olympics, whether in individual or team events.

Jenny Thompson (8) ♂ Swimming
Thompson is an anesthesiologist. She started her medical training in 2000—although she took time out while studying to win further gold World Championship medals.

Katie Ledecky (7) ♂ Swimming
Allyson Felix (7) ♂ Athletics
Amy Van Dyken (6) ♂ Swimming
Dana Vollmer (5) ♂ Swimming
Missy Franklin (5) ♂ Swimming
Sue Bird (5) ♂ Basketball
Diana Taurasi (5) ♂ Basketball
The late Kobe Bryant dubbed Taurasi the "white mamba"; for others she is the G.O.A.T. in women's basketball.

Allison Schmitt (4) ♂ Swimming
Dara Torres (4) ♂ Swimming
Evelyn Ashford (4) ♂ Athletics
Janet Evans (4) ♂ Swimming
Lisa Leslie (4) ♂ Basketball
Pat McCormick (4) ♂ Diving
Sanya Richards-Ross (4) ♂ Athletics
Serena Williams (4) ♂ Tennis
Simone Biles (4) ♂ Gymnastics
Biles's phenomenal medal tally in Olympics and World Championships is greater than any other US gymnast.

Tamika Catchings (4) ♂ Basketball
Teresa Edwards (4) ♂ Basketball
Venus Williams (4) ♂ Tennis

Around the World When You Turned 35

It's a big news day every day, somewhere in the world. Here are the stories that the media thought you'd want to read in the year of your 35th birthday.

- ✦ Prince Charles marries Lady Diana
- ✦ Soviets launch Venera 13 spacecraft
- ✦ Poland declares martial law
- ✦ Pope John Paul II shot
- ✦ London Marathon begins
- ✦ European high-speed rail service begins
- ✦ Yorkshire Ripper is arrested
- ✦ Last country bans slaves
- ✦ Anwar Sadat is assassinated
- ✦ Earthquake hits Athens
- ✦ Riots occur in several UK cities
- ✦ Marcos lifts martial law in the Philippines
- ✦ Attempted coup in Bangladesh
- ✦ Antigua gains independence
- ✦ Passenger ship sinks in Java Sea
- ✦ Pinochet declares himself president of Chile
- ✦ Mitterrand becomes president of France
- ✦ Train disaster kills hundreds in India
- ✦ Israeli jets destroy reactor in Iraq
- ✦ Beirut is bombed by Israel
- ✦ Panda born in Mexico City Zoo
- ✦ Bob Marley dies
- ✦ Belize gains independence
- ✦ Iraq embassy is bombed in Beirut
- ✦ China's population reaches 1 billion

Drinks of the Sixties

For many of those slipping from adolescence into adulthood, your choice of drink says a lot about you. Sophisticated or down-to-earth? A classic, or something to make a statement? In the years that follow, the drinks might change, but the decision remains the same! Here's what was behind a sixties bar.

Falstaff beer

Rusty Nail cocktail
Rumored to be a favorite drink of the Rat Pack.

Hull's Cream Ale
Stinger cocktail
Rheingold Extra Dry Lager
Gunther's Beer
Lone Star Beer
The Gimlet cocktail
The Grasshopper cocktail

Little King's Cream Ale
Best known for its miniature seven-ounce bottles.

Mai Thai cocktail
Genesee Cream Ale

Storz Beer
From Nebraska, Storz was "Brewed for the beer pro."

Iron City Beer
Iron City is reputed to have introduced the first twist-off bottle cap in 1963.

Golden Dream cocktail

Mint Julep cocktail
It's the official drink of the Kentucky Derby, with around 120,000 served over the weekend.

Koch's Light Lager Beer
Arrow 77 Beer
Daiquiri cocktail
Manhattan cocktail
Sterling Premium Pilsner
Carling Black Label
Hamm's Beer
Old fashioned cocktail

Seventies Game Shows

With enough water under the bridge since the 1950s scandals, producers of seventies game shows injected big money into new formats and revamped favorites, some of them screened five nights a week. How many did you cheer on from the couch?

High Rollers 🏆 (1974–88)

Gambit 🏆 (1972–81)

The New Treasure Hunt 🏆 (1973–82)
Perhaps the best-known episode of this show saw a woman faint when she won a Rolls Royce—that she later had to sell in order to pay the taxes.

The Cross-Wits 🏆 (1975–87)

Hollywood Squares 🏆 1966–2004)

The Newlywed Game 🏆 (1966–2013)
Show creator Chuck Barris also made "3's a Crowd"— the show in which men, their secretaries and their wives competed. The public wasn't happy.

Pyramid 🏆 (1973–present)
Thanks to inflation and rival prizes, the $10,000 Pyramid in 1973 didn't last long: from 1976 it was raised in increments to its current peak of $100,000.

Dealer's Choice 🏆 (1974–75)

Sports Challenge 🏆 (1971–79)

Tattletales 🏆 (1974–84)

It's Your Bet 🏆 (1969–73)

Celebrity Sweepstakes 🏆 (1974–77)

Rhyme and Reason 🏆 (1975–76)

Three On A Match 🏆 (1971–74)

The Match Game 🏆 (1962–present)

Sale of the Century 🏆 (1969–89)

The Dating Game 🏆 (1965–99)
The Dating Game—known as Blind Date in many international versions—saw many celebrity appearances before they became well-known, including the Carpenters and Arnold Schwarzenegger.

Popular Boys' Names

40

Just as middle age crept up unnoticed, so the most popular names also evolved. The traditional choices—possibly including yours—are fast losing their appeal to new parents.

Michael

Christopher

Matthew

For fourteen years from 1980, tastes in baby names were locked tight at the top: Michael was the most popular, Christopher was runner-up with Matthew in third spot.

Joshua

David

Daniel

James

Andrew

Robert

John

Ryan

For thirty years from the mid seventies, Ryan's popularity held remarkably steady between 12th and 18th place.

Joseph

Brandon

Justin

William

Jonathan

Nicholas

Jason

Anthony

Brian

Kevin

Eric

Kyle

Adam

Steven

Rising and falling stars:

Austin and Trevor were this year's debutants, while Brent left the Top 100 for good.

Popular Girls' Names

It's a similar story for girls' names. Increasing numbers are taking their infant inspiration from popular culture. The worlds of music, film and theater are all fertile hunting grounds for those in need of inspiration.

Jessica
Ashley
Amanda
Jennifer
Sarah
Stephanie
Nicole
Brittany
Heather
Elizabeth
A name's moment in the sun spans years, sometimes decades. But eventually they disappear out of sight... unless you're Elizabeth. For over a century she's floated between 6th and 26th position.

Megan
Melissa
Amber
Lauren
Rachel
Danielle
Tiffany
Kimberly
Christina
Laura
Samantha
Amy
Michelle
Emily
Rising and falling stars:
Girls we welcomed for the first time this year: Casey, Hannah, Mallory, Alyssa, Felicia, Jasmine and Krista. Names we'd never see in the Top 100 again: Stacy and Stacey, Dominique, Katrina and Karen.

NBA Champions
Since You Were Born

These are the winners of the NBA Finals in your lifetime—
and the number of times they've taken the title.

- Philadelphia Warriors (2)
- Baltimore Bullets (1)
- Minneapolis Lakers (5)
- Rochester Royals (1)
- Syracuse Nationals (1)
- **Boston Celtics (17)**
  1966: After the Lakers won Game 1 of the NBA Finals, the Celtics named their star Bill Russell player-coach. He was the first black coach in the NBA. The Celtics responded by winning the series.

- St. Louis Hawks (1)
- Philadelphia 76ers (2)
- New York Knicks (2)
- Milwaukee Bucks (2)
- **Los Angeles Lakers (12)**
  1980: With Kareem Abdul-Jabbar out with an injury, Lakers' 20-year-old rookie Magic Johnson started at center in the clinching Game 6 and scored 42 points and snared 15 rebounds.

- **Golden State Warriors (4)**
  2015: LeBron James and Stephen Curry, the stars of the teams that faced off in the 2015 NBA Finals, were both born in the same hospital in Akron, Ohio.

- Portland Trail Blazers (1)
- Washington Bullets (1)
- Seattle SuperSonics (1)
- Detroit Pistons (3)
- Chicago Bulls (6)
- Houston Rockets (2)
- San Antonio Spurs (5)
- Miami Heat (3)
- Dallas Mavericks (1)
- Cleveland Cavaliers (1)
- Toronto Raptors (1)

Fashion in the Seventies

The decade that taste forgot? Or a kickback against the sixties and an explosion of individuality? Skirts got shorter (and longer). Block colors and peasant chic vied with sequins and disco glamor. How many of your seventies outfits would you still wear today?

Wrap dresses
Diane von Fürstenberg said she invented the silent, no-zipper wrap dress for one-night stands. "Haven't you ever tried to creep out of the room unnoticed the following morning? I've done that many times."

Tube tops

Midi skirt
In 1970, fashion designers began to lower the hemlines on the mini skirt. This change wasn't welcomed by many consumers. Women picketed in New York City with "stop the midi" signs.

Track suit, running shoes, soccer jerseys
Cowl neck sweaters
His & hers matching outfits
Cork-soled platform shoes
Caftans, Kaftans, Kimonos and mummus
Prairie dresses
Cuban heels
Gaucho pants
Chokers and dog collars as necklaces
Birkenstocks
Tennis headbands
Turtleneck shirts
Puffer vests
Long knit vests layered over tops and pants
Military surplus rucksack bags

"Daisy Dukes" denim shorts
Daisy's revealing cut-off denim shorts in The Dukes of Hazzard caught the attention of network censors. The answer for actor Catherine Bach? Wear flesh-colored pantyhose—just in case.

Yves Saint Laurent
Shrink tops
Bill Gibb

Drinks of the Seventies

Breweries were bigger, and there were fewer of them. Beers were lighter. But what could you (or your parents) serve with your seventies fondue? How about a cocktail that's as heavy on the double-entendre as it was on the sloe gin? Or perhaps match the decade's disco theme with a splash of blue curaçao?

Amber Moon cocktail
Features an unbroken, raw egg and featured in the film Murder on the Orient Express.

Billy Beer

Rainier Beer

Point Special Lager

Tequila Sunrise cocktail

Regal Select Light Beer

Stroh's rum

Long Island Iced Tea cocktail

Merry Widow cocktail

Shell's City Pilsner Premium Beer

Brass Monkey cocktail

The Godfather cocktail

Brown Derby

Sea-Breeze cocktail

Schlitz
This Milwaukee brewery was the country's largest in the late sixties and early seventies. But production problems were followed by a disastrous ad campaign, and by 1981 the original brewery was closed.

Alabama Slammer cocktail

Golden Cadillac cocktail

Harvey Wallbanger cocktail

Red White & Blue Special Lager Beer

Lite Beer from Miller

Coors Banquet Beer
A beer that made the most of its initial limited distribution network by floating the idea of contraband Coors. The idea was so successful that Coors smuggling became central to the plot of the movie Smokey and the Bandit.

US Open Tennis

Across the Open Era and the US National Championship that preceded it, these men won between the year you turned 19 (matching the youngest ever champ, Pete Sampras) and 38 (William Larned's age with his seventh win, in 1911).

1965	Manuel Santana
1966	Fred Stolle
1967	**John Newcombe**

John Newcombe
Newcombe was George W. Bush's drinking companion the day in 1976 when Bush was charged with driving under the influence of alcohol.

1968	Arthur Ashe
1969	Rod Laver
1970	Ken Rosewall
1971	Stan Smith
1972	Illie Nastase
1973	John Newcombe
1974	Jimmy Connors
1975	**Manuel Orantes**

Orantes came back from 5–0 down in the 4th set of the semifinal to win the 4th and 5th sets and upset top-seeded Jimmy Connors in the final.

1976	Jimmy Connors
1977	Guillermo Vilas
1978	**Jimmy Connors**

Connors became the only player to win on all three surfaces that have been used by the US Open.

1979–81	John McEnroe
1982–83	Jimmy Connors
1984	John McEnroe

Books of the Decade

Family, friends, TV, and more: there are as many midlife distractions as there are books on the shelf. Did you get drawn in by these bestsellers, all published in your thirties?

1976	Roots by Alex Haley
1976	The Hite Report by Shere Hite
1977	The Thorn Birds by Colleen McCullough
1977	The Women's Room by Marilyn French
1978	Eye of the Needle by Ken Follett
1978	The World According to Garp by John Irving
1979	Flowers in the Attic by V.C. Andrews
1979	The Hitchhiker's Guide to the Galaxy by Douglas Adams
1979	Sophie's Choice by William Styron
1980	Rage of Angels by Sidney Sheldon
1980	The Bourne Identity by Robert Ludlum
1980	The Covenant by James Michener
1981	The Hotel New Hampshire by John Irving
1981	Noble House by James Clavell
1981	An Indecent Obsession by Colleen McCullough
1982	The Color Purple by Alice Walker
1982	Space by James A. Michener
1983	Pet Sematary by Stephen King
1983	Hollywood Wives by Jackie Collins
1984	You Can Heal Your Life by Louise Hay
1984	Money: A Suicide Note by Martin Amis
1985	The Handmaid's Tale by Margaret Atwood
1985	White Noise by Don DeLillo
1985	Lake Wobegon Days by Garrison Keillor

Around the World When You Turned 40

International stories from farflung places—but did they appear on your radar as you clocked up four decades on the planet?

+ Reactor disaster occurs at Chernobyl
+ Goodwill games begin in Moscow
+ Halley's Comet makes second appearance in 20th century
+ Japanese animation Studio Ghibli releases first film
+ Soviets launch Mir space station
+ Mad cow disease outbreak begins in UK
+ West African volcanic lake releases lethal fumes, killing 1,500
+ South Africa censors news reports
+ Violence erupts in Ireland over Orangemen parades
+ Powerful earthquake hits San Salvador
+ Spain and Portugal join the European Union
+ Newspapers in UK attempt to break strikes
+ Gorbachev begins Glasnost
+ Extensive search for Nessie fails to find "her"
+ Swedish PM is murdered
+ Palestinian uprising begins against Israel
+ Report reveals Israel has nuclear arsenal
+ Micronesia gains independence
+ Argentina wins World Cup in Mexico
+ Plans to create the Channel tunnel are announced
+ UK surgeons perform first triple-organ transplant
+ President Jean-Claude Duvalier flees Haiti
+ Hotel collapse in Singapore kills 33
+ Pope makes historical first visit to synagogue
+ Expo 86 opens in Vancouver

Across the Nation

Here are the headline stories from across the country in the year you hit 40.

- ✦ Space Shuttle Challenger destroyed moments after launch (right)
- ✦ Lazer Tag games begin
- ✦ American Girl dolls released
- ✦ New York Mets win the World Series
- ✦ Chicago Bears become Super Bowl champions
- ✦ Journalist Geraldo Rivera finds Al Capone's vault empty
- ✦ 5 million united for Hands Across America charity event
- ✦ Public transport bans smoking
- ✦ Iran-Contra Affair begins
- ✦ Mike Tyson becomes Heavyweight Champion
- ✦ Tax reform legislation enacted
- ✦ IBM reveals the 12lbs laptop
- ✦ Human Genome Project launched
- ✦ Revolutionary 386 microprocessor introduced
- ✦ Nicotine patch released
- ✦ Statue of Liberty reopens after renovation
- ✦ Postal worker kills 14 fellow workers
- ✦ Rock and Roll Hall of Fame begins inducting musicians
- ✦ Actor Clint Eastwood elected mayor of Carmel, California
- ✦ Singer Tina Turner receives her star on the Walk of Fame
- ✦ Instant replay comes to the NFL
- ✦ President Reagan meets with Soviet's Gorbachev
- ✦ Federal government shuts down because of budget dispute
- ✦ Fox Broadcasting Company begins

Born this year:
- ⚬ Singer Lady Gaga
- ⚬ Actress Lindsay Lohan
- ⚬ American footballer Michael Oher

NASA

Just 73 seconds after the launch of Space Shuttle Challenger on the morning of January 28th, the unimaginable happened. A cold-weather failure of an O-ring seal led to a catastrophe witnessed by millions. Seven astronauts died: Michael Smith, Dick Scobee, Judith Resnik, Ronald McNair, Ellison Onizuka, Gregory Jarvis, and school teacher Christa McAuliffe. To the many children who saw the event, President Reagan told them, "I know it is hard to understand, but sometimes painful things happen ... The Challenger crew was pulling us into the future, and we'll continue to follow them."

The Biggest Hits When You Were 40

Big tunes for a big birthday: how many of them enticed your middle-aged party guests onto the dance floor?

Robert Palmer 🎵 Addicted to Love

Berlin 🎵 Take My Breath Away

Atlantic Starr 🎵 Secret Lovers

Madonna 🎵 Papa Don't Preach

Dionne Warwick and Friends 🎵 That's What Friends Are For

Mister Mister 🎵 Broken Wings

Crystal Gayle 🎵 Cry

Simply Red 🎵 Holding Back the Years

Eddie Money 🎵 Take Me Home Tonight

Lionel Richie 🎵 Say You, Say Me

Hank Williams Jr. 🎵 Ain't Misbehavin'

Janet Jackson 🎵 What Have You Done
for Me Lately

Peter Gabriel 🎵 Sledgehammer

Patti LaBelle
and Michael McDonald 🎵 On My Own

The Georgia Satellites 🎵 Keep Your Hands to Yourself

Steve Winwood 🎵 Higher Love

Timex Social Club 🎵 Rumors

Dan Seals 🎵 Bop

Kenny Loggins 🎵 Danger Zone

The Jets 🎵 Crush on You

Bon Jovi 🎵 You Give Love a Bad Name

Howard Jones 🎵 No One Is to Blame

Run DMC featuring Aerosmith 🎵 Walk This Way

John Cougar Mellencamp 🎵 R.O.C.K. in the USA

Popular Food in the 1970s

From fads to ads, here's a new collection of dinner party dishes and family favorites. This time it's the seventies that's serving up the delights—and some of us are still enjoying them today!

Watergate Salad
Black Forest cake
Chex Mix
Cheese Tid-Bits
Dolly Madison Koo-koos (cupcakes)

Life Cereal
"I'm not gonna try it. You try it. Let's get Mikey...he hates everything." Three on- and off-screen brothers, one memorable ad that ran for much of the seventies.

The Manwich
"A sandwich is a sandwich, but a manwich is a meal," the ads announced in 1969.

Tomato aspic
Bacardi rum cake
Impossible pies
Zucchini bread
Oscar Mayer bologna
Poke Cake made with Jell-O
Libbyland Dinners

Reggie! Bar
Named after New York Yankees' right fielder Reggie Jackson and launched as a novely, Reggie! Bars were on sale for six years.

Hostess Chocodiles
Polynesian chicken salad
Salmon mousse
Cheese log appetizer
Gray Poupon Dijon Mustard

Tootsie Pop
So how many licks does it take to get to the center of a Tootsie Pop? 364, and that's official: it was tested on a "licking machine."

Cars of the 1970s

A decade of strikes, federal regulations, foreign imports, oil crises, safety and quality concerns: car sales were up overall, but the US industry was under pressure like never before. Iconic new models to debut include the Pontiac Firebird and the outrageous, gold-plated Stutz Blackhawk.

1940	**Chrysler New Yorker** When is a New Yorker not a New Yorker? The eighth generation of this upscale car bore little resemblance to the 1940 launch models. Yet in 1970, the New Yorker was barely middle-aged: they lived on until 1997.
1948	Ford F-Series
1959	General Motors Cadillac Coupe de Ville
1959	Chrysler Plymouth Valiant
1960	Chrysler Dodge Dart
1961	**General Motors Oldsmobile Cutlass** The Cutlass outsold any other model in US for four consecutive years, notching up nearly 2 million sales.
1962	General Motors Chevrolet Nova
1965	General Motors Chevrolet Caprice
1965	Ford LTD
1967	General Motors Pontiac Firebird
1968	BMW 2002
1970	Chrysler Dodge Challenger
1970	General Motors Chevrolet Monte Carlo
1970	General Motors Chevrolet Vega
1970	American Motors Corporation Hornet
1970	Ford Maverick
1971	Nissan Datsun 240Z
1971	**Stutz Blackhawk** These luxury automobiles started at a cool $22,000 ($150,000 today); the first car sold went to Elvis. Among the many other celebrity Blackhawk owners was Dean Martin; one of his three models sported the vanity plate DRUNKY. He crashed it.
1971	Ford Pinto
1973	Honda Civic
1975	Ford Granada
1978	Ford Fiesta

US Banknotes

The cast of US banknotes hasn't changed in your lifetime, giving you plenty of time to get to know them. (Although if you have a lot of pictures of James Madison and Salmon P. Chase around the house, you might want to think about a visit to the bank.)

Fifty cent paper coin (1862-1876) 🔳 Abraham Lincoln
These bills were known as "shinplasters" because the quality of the paper was so poor that they could be used to bandage leg wounds during the Civil War.

One dollar bill (1862-1869) 🔳 Salmon P. Chase
The US Secretary of Treasury during Civil War, Salmon P. Chase is credited with putting the phrase "In God we trust" on US currency beginning in 1864.

One dollar bill (1869-present) 🔳 George Washington
Some bills have a star at the end of the serial number. This means they are replacement bills for those printed with errors.

One silver dollar certificate (1886-96) 🔳 Martha Washington

Two dollar bill (1862-present) 🔳 Thomas Jefferson
Two dollar bills have a reputation of being rare, but there are actually 600 million in circulation in the US.

Five dollar bill (1914-present) 🔳 Abraham Lincoln
Ten dollar bill (1914-1929) 🔳 Andrew Jackson
Ten dollar bill (1929-present) 🔳 Alexander Hamilton
Twenty dollar bill (1865-1869) 🔳 Pocahontas
Twenty dollar bill (1914-1929) 🔳 Grover Cleveland
Twenty dollar bill (1929-present) 🔳 Andrew Jackson
Fifty dollar bill (1914-present) 🔳 Ulysses S. Grant

One hundred dollar bill (1914-1929) 🔳 Benjamin Franklin
The one hundred dollar bill has an expected circulation life of 22.9 years while the one dollar bill has an expected circulation life of just 6.6 years.

Five hundred dollar bill (1918-1928) 🔳 John Marshall
Five hundred dollar bill (1945-1969) 🔳 William McKinley
One thousand dollar bill (1918-1928) 🔳 Alexander Hamilton
One thousand dollar bill (1928-1934) 🔳 Grover Cleveland
Five thousand dollar bill (1918-1934) 🔳 James Madison
Ten thousand dollar bill (1928-1934) 🔳 Salmon P. Chase

Male Olympic Gold Medalists in Your Lifetime

These are the male athletes that have scooped the greatest number of individual and team gold medals at the Summer Olympics in your lifetime.

Michael Phelps (23) 🏅 Swimming (right)

Carl Lewis (9) 🏅 Athletics

Mark Spitz (9) 🏅 Swimming

For 36 years, Spitz's 7-gold-medal haul at the 1972 Munich Olympics was unbeaten; Michael Phelps finally broke the spell with his eighth gold in Beijing.

Matt Biondi (8) 🏅 Swimming

Caeleb Dressel (7) 🏅 Swimming

Ryan Lochte (6) 🏅 Swimming

Don Schollander (5) 🏅 Swimming

Gary Hall Jr. (5) 🏅 Swimming

Aaron Peirsol (5) 🏅 Swimming

Nathan Adrian (5) 🏅 Swimming

Tom Jager (5) 🏅 Swimming

Al Oerter Jr. (4) 🏅 Athletics

Four out of four: Oerter won Olympic gold medals in the discus in every Games from 1956–1968. He fought injuries that required him to wear a neck brace for the 1964 Tokyo Olympics—but he still set an Olympic record.

Greg Louganis (4) 🏅 Diving

Jason Lezak (4) 🏅 Swimming

John Naber (4) 🏅 Swimming

Jon Olsen (4) 🏅 Swimming

Lenny Krayzelburg (4) 🏅 Swimming

Matt Grevers (4) 🏅 Swimming

Michael Johnson (4) 🏅 Athletics

Once the fastest man in the world over 200 meters, Johnson took 15 minutes to walk the same distance in 2018 following a mini-stroke—but took it as a sign that he'd make a full recovery.

Harrison Dillard (4) 🏅 Athletics

Dillard—known as "Bones" for his skinny build—aspired to match the feats of his idol, Jesse Owens. And he did, becoming the only man to win gold as a sprinter and a hurdler.

Between 2000 and 2016, Michael Phelps won 28 Olympic medals, including 23 gold and 16 for individual events. That's 10 more than his nearest competitor, Larisa Latynina, a gymnast of the Soviet Union who took her last gold medal fifty years earlier.

Winter Olympics Venues Since You Were Born

Unless you're an athlete or winter sports fan, the Winter Olympics can slip past almost unnoticed. These are the venues; can you remember the host countries and years?

Lillehammer
Cortina d'Ampezzo
Oslo
Salt Lake City
Sapporo
Albertville
The last Games to be held in the same year as the Summer Olympics, with the next Winter Olympics held two years later.

Turin
Grenoble
Beijing
Sarajevo
Lake Placid
Sochi
Innsbruck (twice)
This usually snowy city experienced its mildest winter in 60 years; the army transported snow and ice from the mountains. Nevertheless, twelve years later, the Winter Olympics were back.

Squaw Valley
Nagano
St Moritz
The first Winter Olympics to be held for 12 years and named the 'Games of Renewal'; Japan and Germany were not invited.

Calgary
Vancouver
PyeongChang

Answers: Lillehammer: Norway, 1994; Cortina d'Ampezzo: Italy, 1956; Oslo: Norway, 1952; Salt Lake City: USA, 2002; Sapporo: Japan, 1972; Albertville: France, 1992; Turin: Italy, 2006; Grenoble: France, 1968; Beijing: China, 2022; Sarajevo: Yugoslavia, 1984; Lake Placid: USA, 1980; Sochi: Russia, 2014; Innsbruck: Austria, 1964; Squaw Valley: USA, 1960; Nagano: Japan, 1998; St Moritz: Switzerland, 1948; Calgary: Canada, 1988; Innsbruck: Austria, 1976; Vancouver: Canada, 2010; PyeongChang: South Korea, 2018

Fashion in the Eighties

Eighties fashion was many things, but subtle wasn't one of them. Influences were everywhere from aerobics to Wall Street, from pop princesses to preppy polo shirts. The result was chaotic, but fun. How many eighties throwbacks still lurk in your closet?

Stirrup pants
Ralph Lauren
Ruffled shirts
Jean Paul Gaultier
Acid wash jeans
Stone washing had been around a while, but the acid wash trend came about by chance—Rifle jeans of Italy accidentally tumbled jeans, bleach, and pumice stone with a little water. The result? A fashion craze was born.

Camp collar shirt with horizontal stripes
Thierry Mugler
Oversized denim jackets
Scrunchies
"Members Only" jackets
Members Only military-inspired jackets were marketed with the tagline "When you put it on...something happens."

Paper bag waist pants
Pleated stonewash baggy jeans
Cut-off sweatshirts/hoodies
Vivienne Westwood
Azzedine Alaia
Shoulder pads
Dookie chains
Leg warmers
Bally shoes
Jordache jeans
Calvin Klein
Windbreaker jackets
Ray-Ban Wayfarer sunglasses
Popularized by Tom Cruise in the movie Risky Business.
Parachute pants
Jumpsuits

World Buildings

Some of the most striking and significant buildings in the world sprang up when you were between 25 and 50 years old. How many do you know?

1971	Näsinneula tower, Tampere, Finland
1972	Olympiastadion, Munich
1973	**The Sydney Opera House**

The iconic Sydney Opera House sits on the tip of Bennelong Point—on a site that previously homed a tram shed.

1974	Shinjuku Mitsui Building, Tokyo
1975	First Canadian Place, Toronto
1976	The CN Tower, Toronto
1977	**The Centre Pompidou, Paris**

The Centre Pompidou, known locally as Beaubourg, is considered the "inside-out" landmark—its structure and mechanical services are outside the building.

1978	Sunshine 60, Tokyo
1979	Kuwait Towers, Kuwait City
1980	Hopewell Centre, Hong Kong
1981	Sydney Tower
1983	Teresa Carreño Cultural Complex, Caracas
1984	Deutsche Bank Twin Towers, Frankfurt
1985	Exchange Square, Hong Kong
1986	**Baha'i Lotus Temple, New Delhi**

The Lotus Temple is open to all faiths to come worship, but no images, pictures, sermons, or even musical instruments are permitted.

1988	Canterra Tower, Calgary
1989	The Louvre Pyramid, Paris
1990	Bank of China Tower, Hong Kong
1991	One Canada Square, London
1992	Central Plaza, Hong Kong
1995	Republic Plaza, Singapore
1996	**Petronas Twin Towers, Kuala Lampur**

As iconic in Malaysia as the Eiffel Tower is in France. Its skybridge is actually two stories and is the highest of its kind in the world.

Kentucky Derby Winners

These are the equine and human heroes from the "most exciting two minutes of sport" during your thirties and forties. Did any of them make you rich?

1976	Bold Forbes (Angel Cordero Jr.)
1977	Seattle Slew (Jean Cruguet)
1978	**Affirmed (Steve Cauthen)** Affirmed won the Triple Crown, with Alydar finishing second in all three Triple Crown races.
1979	Spectacular Bid (Ronnie Franklin)
1980	**Genuine Risk (Jacinto Vasquez)** Genuine Risk became the first female horse to win the Kentucky Derby since 1915.
1981	Pleasant Colony (Jorge Velasquez)
1982	Gato Del Sol (Eddie Delahoussaye)
1983	Sunny's Halo (Eddie Delahoussaye)
1984	Swale (Laffit Pincay Jr.)
1985	Spend A Buck (Angel Cordero Jr.)
1986	**Ferdinand (Bill Shoemaker)** 54-year-old Bill Shoemaker became the oldest jockey to ever win the Kentucky Derby.
1987	Alysheba (Chris McCarron)
1988	Winning Colors (Gary Stevens)
1989	Sunday Silence (Pat Valenzuela)
1990	Unbridled (Craig Perret)
1991	Strike the Gold (Chris Antley)
1992	Lil E. Tee (Pat Day)
1993	Sea Hero (Jerry Bailey)
1994	Go for Gin (Chris McCarron)
1995	Thunder Gulch (Gary Stevens)
1996	Grindstone (Jerry Bailey)

World Series Champions Since You Were Born

These are the winners of the Commissioner's Trophy and the number of times they've been victorious in your lifetime.

- Detroit Tigers (2)
- New York Yankees (17)
- Cincinnati Reds (3)
- St. Louis Cardinals (5)
- Cleveland Indians (1)
- New York Giants (1)
- Brooklyn Dodgers (1)
- Milwaukee Braves (1)
- **Los Angeles Dodgers (6)**
  1988: Dodgers' Kirk Gibson, battling injuries, hit a game-winning home run in his only at-bat of the 1988 World Series.
- Pittsburgh Pirates (3)
- Baltimore Orioles (3)
- **New York Mets (2)**
  1969: The Mets had never finished above 9th in their division.
- Oakland Athletics (4)
- Philadelphia Phillies (2)
- Kansas City Royals (2)
- **Minnesota Twins (2)**
  1991: Both teams had finished in last place the previous season.
- Toronto Blue Jays (2)
- Atlanta Braves (2)
- Florida Marlins (2)
- Arizona Diamondbacks (1)
- Anaheim Angels (1)
- Boston Red Sox (4)
- Chicago White Sox (1)
- San Francisco Giants (3)
- **Chicago Cubs (1)**
  2016: The Cubs' first World Series win since 1908.
- Houston Astros (1)
- Washington Nationals (1)

Books of the Decade

By our forties, most of us have decided what we like to read. But occasionally a book can break the spell, revealing the delights of other genres. Did any of these newly published books do that for you?

1986	It by Stephen King
1986	Wanderlust by Danielle Steele
1987	Patriot Games by Tom Clancy
1987	Beloved by Toni Morrison
1987	The Bonfire of the Vanities by Tom Wolfe
1988	The Cardinal of the Kremlin by Tom Clancy
1988	The Sands of Time by Sidney Sheldon
1989	Clear and Present Danger by Stephen R. Covey
1989	The Pillars of the Earth by Ken Follett
1990	The Plains of Passage by Jean M. Auel
1990	Possession by A.S. Byatt
1990	Four Past Midnight by Stephen King
1991	The Firm by John Grisham
1991	The Kitchen God's Wife by Amy Tan
1991	Scarlett by Alexandra Ripley
1992	The Bridges of Madison County by Robert James Waller
1992	The Secret History by Donna Tartt
1993	The Celestine Prophecy by James Redfield
1993	Like Water for Chocolate by Laura Esquivel
1994	The Chamber by John Grisham
1994	Disclosure by Michael Crichton
1995	The Horse Whisperer by Nicholas Evans
1995	The Lost World by Michael Crichton
1995	The Rainmaker by John Grisham

Vice Presidents in Your Lifetime

The linchpin of a successful presidency, the best springboard to become POTUS, or both? Here are the men—and woman—who have shadowed the most powerful person in the world in your lifetime.

1949-53	**Alben W. Barkley** Barkley died of a heart attack during a convention speech three years after the end of his term.
1953-61	Richard Nixon
1961-63	Lyndon B. Johnson
1965-69	**Hubert Humphrey** Christmas 1977: with just weeks to live, the former VP to President Johnson made goodbye calls. One was to Richard Nixon, the man who had beaten Humphrey to become president in 1968. Sensing Nixon's unhappiness at his status as Washington outcast, Humphrey invited him to take a place of honor at a funeral he knew was fast approaching.
1969-73	**Spiro Agnew (right)**
1973-74	Gerald Ford
1974-77	Nelson Rockefeller
1977-81	Walter Mondale
1981-89	**George H. W. Bush** He is only the second vice president to win the presidency while holding the office of vice president.
1989-93	**Dan Quayle** Quayle famously misspelled potato ("potatoe")
1993-2001	**Al Gore** This VP won the Nobel Peace Prize in 2007, following in the footsteps of two other former vice presidents.
2001-09	Dick Cheney
2009-17	Joe Biden
2017-20	**Mike Pence** In the 90s, Pence took a break from politics to become a conservative radio talk show and television host.
2020-	Kamala Harris

Spiro Agnew resigned in 1973, the second VP to quit in America's history (the first was John Calhoun in 1932). He stepped down after being charged with tax evasion and taking bribes. He covered his legal debts with a loan from friend Frank Sinatra. In 1983 he was compelled to repay $268,000: the money he had taken in bribes, plus interest.

British Prime Ministers in Your Lifetime

These are the occupants of 10 Downing Street, London, during your lifetime (not including Larry the resident cat). Don't be deceived by that unassuming black (blast-proof) door: Number 10 features a warren of more than 100 rooms.

1945–51	Clement Attlee
1951–55	**Sir Winston Churchill** Churchill was made an honorary citizen of the United States in 1963, one of only eight to receive this honor.
1955–57	Sir Anthony Eden
1957–63	**Harold Macmillan** Macmillan was the scion of a wealthy publishing family. He resigned following a scandal in which a minister was found to have lied about his relationship with a 19-year-old model. Macmillan died aged 92; his last words were, "I think I will go to sleep now."
1963–64	Sir Alec Douglas-Home
1964–70	Harold Wilson
1970–74	Edward Heath
1974–76	Harold Wilson
1976–79	James Callaghan
1979–90	**Margaret Thatcher** In 1994, Thatcher was working late in a Brighton hotel, preparing a conference speech. A bomb—planted weeks earlier by the IRA five stories above—detonated, devastating the hotel. Five were killed; Thatcher was unscathed. The conference went ahead.
1990–97	John Major
1997–2007	Tony Blair
2007–10	**Gordon Brown** Brown has no sight in his left eye after being kicked in a school rugby game; in 2009, while Prime Minister, tears in the right retina were also diagnosed.
2010–16	David Cameron
2016–19	Theresa May
2019–	Boris Johnson

Things People Do Now (Part 2)

Imagine your ten-year-old self being given this list of today's mundane tasks and habits—and the puzzled look on your face!

- ✦ Listen to a podcast
- ✦ Go "viral" or become social media famous
- ✦ Watch YouTube
- ✦ Track the exact location of family members via your smartphone
- ✦ Watch college football playoffs
- ✦ Have drive-thru fast food delivered to your door
- ✦ Check reviews before trying a new restaurant or product
- ✦ Use LED light bulbs to save on your electric bill
- ✦ Wear leggings as pants for any occasion
- ✦ Use hashtags (#) to express an idea or show support
- ✦ Join a CrossFit gym
- ✦ Use a Forever stamp to send a letter
- ✦ Carry a reusable water bottle
- ✦ Work for a company with an "unlimited" paid time off policy
- ✦ "Binge" a TV show
- ✦ Marry a person of the same sex
- ✦ Take your shoes off when going through airport security
- ✦ Take a selfie
- ✦ Use tooth-whitening strips
- ✦ Feed babies and kids from food pouches
- ✦ Buy recreational marijuana from a dispensary (in some states)
- ✦ Store documents "in the cloud" and work on them from any device
- ✦ Clean up after your pets using compostable waste bags
- ✦ Buy free-range eggs and meat at the grocery store

A Lifetime of Technology

It's easy to lose sight of the breadth and volume of life-enhancing technology that became commonplace during the 20th Century. Here are some of the most notable advances to be made in the years you've been an adult.

1967	Hand-held calculator
1968	Virtual Reality
1969	Laser printer
1971	Email
1972	Video games console (Magnavox Odyssey)
1973	Mobile phone
1974	Universal Product Code
1979	Compact disc
1982	**Emoticons** The inventor of the smiley emoticon hands out "Smiley" cookies every September 19th—the anniversary of the first time it was used.
1983	Internet
1986	Mir Space Station
1988	**Internet virus** The first Internet worm was specifically designed to crack passwords. Its inventor was the son of the man who invented computer passwords.
1989	World Wide Web
1992	Digital hand-sized mobile phone
1994	Bluetooth
1995	**Mouse with scroll wheel** Mouse scroll wheels were developed primarily as a zoom function for large Excel sheets, but became more useable as a means of scrolling.
1998	Google
1999	Wi-Fi
2000	Camera phone
2001	Wikipedia
2004	Facebook
2007	Apple iPhone
2009	Bitcoin
2014	Amazon Alexa

The Biggest Hits
When You Were 50

Fifty: an age when your musical taste is largely settled and modern music can lose its appeal…but how many do you know and how many do you like?

The Smashing Pumpkins ♪ 1979

Los del Rio ♪ Macarena

Celine Dion ♪ Because You Loved Me

Metallica ♪ Until It Sleeps

Tracy Chapman ♪ Give Me One Reason

The Fugees ♪ Killing Me Softly with His Song

The Spice Girls ♪ Wannabe

LeAnn Rimes ♪ Blue

Toni Braxton ♪ You're Makin' Me High

Collective Soul ♪ The World I Know

Eric Clapton ♪ Change the World

Patty Loveless ♪ You Can Feel Bad

Oasis ♪ Champagne Supernova

No Doubt ♪ Don't Speak

Blues Traveler ♪ Hook

Mindy McCready ♪ Guys Do It All the Time

Blackstreet featuring Dr. Dre ♪ No Diggity

Primitive Radio Gods ♪ Standing Outside a Broken Phone Booth with Money in My Hand

Brooks and Dunn ♪ My Maria

R. Kelly ♪ I Believe I Can Fly

Dave Matthews Band ♪ Crash Into Me

Jewel ♪ Who Will Save Your Soul

George Strait ♪ Blue Clear Sky

BoDeans ♪ Closer to Free

Grand Constructions

Governments around the world spent much of the 20th century nation building (and rebuilding), with huge civil engineering projects employing new construction techniques. Here are some of the biggest built between the ages of 25 and 50.

1971	Azadi Tower, Iran
1972	Snowy Mountains Scheme, Australia
1973	Chesapeake Bay Bridge, US
1974	Charles de Gaulle Airport, France
1975	Orange-Fish River Tunnel, South Africa
1976	**Sonnenberg Tunnel, Switzerland** A 5,000-ft road tunnel built to double up as a 20,000-capacity nuclear shelter. Blast doors weigh 350 tons... but take 24 hours to close.
1977	Guoliang Tunnel, China
1978	West Gate Bridge, Australia
1979	Genting Sempah Tunnel, Malaysia
1980	Reichsbrücke, Austria
1982	Abu Dhabi International Airport, Abu Dhabi
1983	Queen Alia International Airport, Jordan
1984	Tennessee-Tombigbee Waterway, US
1985	Penang Bridge, Malaysia
1986	National Waterway 1, India
1987	Pikeville Cut-Through, US
1988	Great Seto Bridge, Japan
1989	Skybridge (TransLink), Canada
1991	Fannefjord Tunnel, Norway
1992	Vidyasagar Setu Bridge, India
1993	Rainbow Bridge, Japan
1994	**English Channel tunnel, UK & France** Even at its predicted cost of $7 billion, the longest underwater tunnel in the world was already the most expensive project ever. By the time it opened, the bill was more than $13 billion.
1995	Denver International Airport, US
1996	Tenerife International Centre for Trade Fairs and Congresses, Spain

Popular Food in the 1980s

The showy eighties brought us food to dazzle and delight. Food to make us feel good, food to share and food to go. Some innovations fell by the wayside, but many more can still be found in our baskets forty years later.

Hot Pockets
Hot Pockets were the brainchild of two brothers, originally from Iran. Their invention was launched as the Tastywich before being tweaked to become the Hot Pockets enjoyed by millions.

Bagel Bites

Crystal Light

Steak-Umms

Sizzlean Bacon

Potato skins appetizers

Tofutti ice cream

Hi-C Ecto Cooler
Hi-C has been around for a very long time, but the Ecto Cooler dates back to the Ghostbusters movie hype of the 1980s.

Hot buttered O's

Knorr Spinach Dip

Original New York Seltzer

Blondies

Blackened Redfish
The trend for blackening redfish prompted fish stocks to drop so low that commercial fishing for the species was banned in Louisiana.

Bartles & Jaymes Wine Coolers

Fruit Wrinkles

Stuffed mushrooms appetizers

TCBY Frozen Yogurt
TCBY originally stood for "This Can't Be Yogurt."

Sushi

Fajitas

Capri Sun

Jell-O Pudding Pops

Lean Cuisine frozen meals
Lean Cuisine is an FDA-regulated term, so all Lean Cuisine frozen meals need to be within the limit for saturated fat and cholesterol.

Eighties Symbols of Success

In the flamboyant era of Dallas and Dynasty there were many ways to show that you, too, had really made it. Forty years on, it's fascinating to see how some of these throwbacks are outdated or available to nearly everyone, while others are still reserved for today's wealthy peacocks.

BMW car

Cellular car phone

Rolex watch

Cosmetic surgery

In 1981 there were 1,000 liposuction procedures performed. That number increased to 250,000 by 1989.

VCR

"Home theater" projection TV

In-ground pool

AKC-registered dog

McMansion

Pagers/"beeper"

Aprica stroller

Home intercom system

Heart-shaped Jacuzzi tub

NordicTrack

This machine was originally called the Nordic Jock but was renamed due to compaints from women's rights groups.

Cruise vacation

Restaurant-standard kitchen appliances

A popular commercial stove produced enough heat to warm an average three-bedroom home. It was the energy equivalent of six residential stoves.

Ronald Reagan-style crystal jelly bean jar on your desk

Apple or Commodore 64 home computer

Volvo Station Wagon

Gordon Gekko-style "power suit"

Owning a horse or riding lessons for your children

Private jet

Tennis bracelet

Monogrammed clothes and accessories

Mary Evans/Classic Stock/K. Vreeland

Launched in 1980, the Apple III personal computer seen here went on sale for a hefty $4,000 and up, the equivalent of over $13,000 today. It didn't sell well and was soon withdrawn (unlike the Apple II, which went on to sell more than 5 million units).

The Transportation Coils

This novel issue of more than 50 definitive stamps first appeared on post in the early eighties, and became a favorite of collectors for its mono color engraved images of transportation methods past and present. Stamps carrying the printing plate number are particularly treasured. Here's a selection you may remember.

1 c ▦ Omnibus

2 c ▦ Locomotive

3 c ▦ Handcar

4 c ▦ **Stagecoach**

Coaches have been ferrying people and mail between US towns and cities since the late 18th century.

5 c ▦ Motorcycle

5.5c ▦ **Star Route Truck**

Star routes were 19th century mail routes on which carriers bid to make deliveries.

6 c ▦ Tricycle

7.4 c ▦ Baby Buggy

10 c ▦ Canal Boat

11 c ▦ Caboose

12.5 c ▦ Pushcart

13 c ▦ Patrol Wagon

15 c ▦ Tugboat

17 c ▦ Electric Auto

17 c ▦ Dog Sled

17.5 c ▦ Racing car

18 c ▦ Surrey

20 c ▦ Cog Railway

21 c ▦ Railway Mail Car

23 c ▦ Lunch Wagon

24.1 c ▦ Tandem Bike

25 c ▦ Bread Wagon

32 c ▦ Ferry Boat

$1 ▦ **Sea Plane**

The US Navy bought its first sea plane in 1911: a Curtiss Model E, with a range of 150 miles.

Eighties Game Shows

By the eighties, game shows had their work cut out to compete against the popularity of new drama and talk shows. Still, an injection of celebrity glamour and dollar bills—alongside hours to be filled on new cable TV channels—ensured their survival. Here are the biggies.

Double Dare 🏆 (1986-2019)
Remote Control 🏆 (1987-90)
Scrabble 🏆 (1984-93)
The Price Is Right 🏆 (1972-present)
"Come on down!"—perhaps the best-known game show catchphrase of all time. One 2008 contestant was even happier than usual to do just that after 3 chips dropped into the Plinko all hit the $10,000 jackpot. Fluke? No, wires used to rig the result when filming ads hadn't been removed. She was allowed to keep the $30,000.

Family Feud 🏆 (1976-present)
Press Your Luck 🏆 (1983-86)
A show perhaps best remembered for the contestant Michael Larson, who memorized the game board and engineered a winning streak worth over $110,000. It wasn't cheating—Larson kept the winnings—but the game was swiftly reformulated.

Chain Reaction 🏆 1980-present)
Blockbusters 🏆 (1980-87)
Win, Lose, or Draw 🏆 (1987-90)
On The Spot 🏆 (1984-88)
Jeopardy! 🏆 (1964-present)
Card Sharks 🏆 (1978-present)
Wheel of Fortune 🏆 (1975-present)
Hostess Vanna White is estimated to clap 600 times a show; that's around 4,000,000 times since she began in 1982.

Fandango 🏆 (1983-88)
Body Language 🏆 (1984-86)
Jackpot! 🏆 (1974-90)

Popular Boys' Names

Not many of these boys' names were popular when you were born. But how many more of them are now in your twenty-first century family?

Jacob

Michael

Joshua

Joshua is very much a turn-of-the-century kind of name. He entered the Top 100 in 1972 and climbed to spend 25 years inside the top 5; now, he rarely makes the top 50.

Ethan

Matthew

Daniel

Andrew

Christopher

Anthony

William

Joseph

Alexander

David

Ryan

Noah

James

Nicholas

Tyler

John

Logan

Christian

Jonathan

Nathan

Benjamin

Samuel

Dylan

Rising and falling stars:

Liam is the only new entrant to the Top 100; Alejandro and Richard won't be seen again after 2006.

Popular Girls' Names

It's a similar story for girls' names: only Elizabeth featured in the 30 most popular names for your year of birth. How long will it be before we turn full circle and Shirley, Patricia and Barbara make a comeback?

Emily
Emily has held the top slot for 12 years since 1900—more than most. Though nobody comes close to Mary (54 years). Others: Linda (6), Lisa (8), Jennifer (15), Jessica (9), Ashley (2), Emma (6), Isabella (2), Sophia (3) and Olivia (since 2019).

Emma
Madison
Isabella
Ava
Abigail
Olivia
Hannah
Sophia
Samantha
Elizabeth
Ashley
Mia
Alexis
Sarah
Grace
Natalie
Chloe
Alyssa
Brianna
Ella

Addison
In 28th position, Addison was the highest placed new Top 100 name of the last 120 years.

Rising and falling stars:
Say hello to Valeria, Aubrey, Natalia, Gianna, Jayla and Layla. Wave goodbye to Jenna, Rebecca and Jordan.

Game Show Hosts of the Seventies and Eighties

Here is the new generation of hosts: bow-tied, wide-smiled men to steer family favorites through tumultuous times. Astonishingly, one or two are still holding the cards.

John Charles Daly ➤◄ What's My Line (1950–1967)

Garry Moore ➤◄ To Tell The Truth (1969–1976)

Chuck Woolery ➤◄ Love Connection (1983–1994)

Bob Barker ➤◄ The Price Is Right (1972–2007)

Pat Sajak ➤◄ Wheel of Fortune (1981–)
Sajak took the crown for the longest-reigning game-show host of all time in 1983, when his 35-year reign surpassed that of Bob Barker as host of The Price is Right.

Peter Tomarken ➤◄ Press Your Luck (1983–86)

Gene Rayburn ➤◄ The Match Game (1962–1981)

Alex Trebek ➤◄ Jeopardy! (1984–2020)
At the time of his death in 2020, Trebek had hosted more than 8,200 episodes of the show.

Dick Clark ➤◄ Pyramid (1973–1988)

Richard Dawson ➤◄ Family Feud (1976–1995)

Peter Marshall ➤◄ Hollywood Squares (1966–1981)

Howard Cosell ➤◄ Battle of the Network Stars (1976–1988)

Marc Summers ➤◄ Double Dare (1986–1993)

Tom Kennedy ➤◄ Name That Tune (1974–1981)

Bert Convy ➤◄ Tattletales (1974–78; 1982–84)

Ken Ober ➤◄ Remote Control (1987–1990)

Jim Lange ➤◄ The Dating Game (1965–1980)

Wink Martindale ➤◄ Tic-Tac-Dough (1978–1985)

Art Fleming ➤◄ Jeopardy! (1964–1975; 1978–79)
Host for the original version, Fleming declined to host the comeback in 1983. His friend Pat Sajak took the job.

Jack Narz ➤◄ Concentration (1973–78)

Dennis James ➤◄ The Price Is Right (1972–77)

Jim Perry ➤◄ $ale of the Century (1983–89)

John Davidson ➤◄ Hollywood Squares (1986–89)

Ray Combs ➤◄ Family Feud (1988–1994)

Mike Adamle ➤◄ American Gladiators (1989–1996)

TV News Anchors of the Seventies and Eighties

The explosion in cable channels that began with CNN in 1980 brought a host of fresh presenters to join the ranks of trusted personalities that bring us the news. How many of them do you remember?

Dan Rather ♟ (CBS)
"Kenneth, what's the frequency?" Those were the words of the man who attacked Rather in 1986. It took a decade before the message was decoded; his assailant wanted to block the beams he believed TV networks were using to target him.

Peter Jennings ♟ (ABC)
Tom Brokaw ♟ (NBC)
Ted Koppel ♟ (ABC)
Bill Beutel ♟ (ABC)
Jessica Savitch ♟ (NBC)
Connie Chung ♟ (NBC)
Diane Sawyer ♟ (CBS/ABC)
Sam Donaldson ♟ (ABC)
Barbara Walters ♟ (ABC)
Walters was a popular pioneer; the first woman to co-host and anchor news programs, reaching 74 million viewers with her interview of Monica Lewinsky.

Frank Reynolds ♟ (ABC)
Jane Pauley ♟ (NBC)
Roger Grimsby ♟ (ABC)
Roger Mudd ♟ (CBS/NBC)
Garrick Utley ♟ (NBC)
Bernard Shaw ♟ (CNN)
Frank McGee ♟ (NBC)
Ed Bradley ♟ (CBS)
Larry King ♟ (CNN)
Kathleen Sullivan ♟ (ABC/CBS/NBC)
Jim Lehrer ♟ (PBS)
Robert MacNeil ♟ (PBS)
In 1963, MacNeil had a brief exchange of words with a man leaving the Texas School Book Depository; to this day, it is uncertain whether this was Lee Harvey Oswald.

FIFA World Cup: Down to the Last Four in Your Life

Here are the teams that have made the last four of the world's most watched sporting event in your lifetime (last year in brackets). The US men's team has reached the semifinals once, back in 1930.

France ⚽ (2018, winner)
Croatia ⚽ (2018, runner-up)
During a 2006 match against Australia, Croatian player Josip Šimunić was booked three times due to a referee blunder.

Belgium ⚽ (2018, 3rd)
England ⚽ (2018, 4th)
In the run-up to the 1966 World Cup, hosted and won by England, the trophy was held to ransom. An undercover detective with fake banknotes arrested the crook; a dog named Pickles found the trophy under a bush.

Brazil ⚽ (2014, 4th)
Germany ⚽ (2014, winner)
Argentina ⚽ (2014, runner-up)
Netherlands ⚽ (2014, 3rd)
Spain ⚽ (2010, winner)
Uruguay ⚽ (2010, 4th)
Italy ⚽ (2006, winner)
Portugal ⚽ (2006, 4th)
Turkey ⚽ (2002, 3rd)
Korean Republic ⚽ (2002, 4th)
Sweden ⚽ (1994, 3rd)
Bulgaria ⚽ (1994, 4th)
Poland ⚽ (1982, 3rd)
Russia ⚽ (1966, 4th)
Czech Republic (as Czechoslovakia) ⚽ (1962, runner-up)
Chile ⚽ (1962, 3rd)
The 1962 World Cup saw the 'Battle of Santiago' between Chile and Italy. The first foul occurred 12 seconds into the game, a player was punched in the nose, and police intervened several times.

Serbia (as Yugoslavia) ⚽ (1962, 4th)
Hungary ⚽ (1954, runner-up)
Austria ⚽ (1954, third)

Books of the Decade

Our final decade of books are the bookstore favorites from your fifties. How many did you read…and can you remember the plot, or the cover?

1996	Angela's Ashes by Frank McCourt
1996	Bridget Jones's Diary by Helen Fielding
1996	Infinite Jest by David Foster Wallace
1997	American Pastoral by Philip Roth
1997	Tuesdays with Morrie by Mitch Albom
1998	The Poisonwood Bible by Barbara Kingsolver
1998	A Man in Full by Tom Wolfe
1999	The Testament by John Grisham
1999	Hannibal by Thomas Harris
1999	Girl with a Pearl Earring by Tracy Chevalier
2000	Angels & Demons by Dan Brown
2000	Interpreter of Maladies by Jhumpa Lahiri
2000	White Teeth by Zadie Smith
2001	Life of Pi by Yann Martel
2001	The Corrections by Jonathan Franzen
2002	Everything is Illuminated by Jonathan Safran Foer
2002	The Lovely Bones by Alice Sebold
2003	The Da Vinci Code by Dan Brown
2003	The Kite Runner by Khaled Hosseini
2004	The Five People You Meet in Heaven by Mitch Albom
2004	Cloud Atlas by David Mitchell
2005	Never Let Me Go by Kazuo Ishiguro
2005	The Book Thief by Markus Zusak
2005	Twilight by Stephanie Meyer

April 17, 1970: Jim Lovell is brought aboard a helicopter—the last of the
three astronauts from the Apollo 13 mission to be lifted from the floating

Apollo Astronauts

Whatever your personal memories of the events, the moon landings are now woven into our national story—but not all of the Apollo astronauts who made the journey are equally well known. Twelve landed; twelve remained in lunar orbit. Gus Grissom, Ed White, and Roger B Chaffee died in training.

Landed on the moon:

Alan Bean

Alan Shepard

Shepard was the oldest person to walk on the moon at age 47.

Buzz Aldrin

Charles Duke

David Scott

Edgar Mitchell

Eugene Cernan

Harrison Schmitt

James Irwin

John Young

Neil Armstrong

Pete Conrad

Remained in low orbit:

Al Worden

Bill Anders

Anders took the iconic "Earthrise" photo.

Dick Gordon

Frank Borman

Fred Haise

Jack Swigert

Jim Lovell

Ken Mattingly

Michael Collins

Ron Evans

Made the final spacewalk of the program to retrieve film cassettes.

Stuart Roosa

On the Apollo 14 mission he carried seeds from 5 species of trees. They were planted across the US and are known as "Moon Trees."

Tom Stafford

US Open Tennis

And now it's the women's turn. Here are the tournament's victors when you were between the ages of the current "winning window": 16 years (Tracy Austin in 1979), and a venerable 42 years (Molla Mallory in 1926: she won eight times).

1962	Margaret Court
1963–64	Maria Bueno
1965	Margaret Court
1966	Maria Bueno
1967	Billie Jean King
1968	Virginia Wade
1969–70	**Margaret Court** Court won both the amateur and open championships in 1969.
1971–72	Billie Jean King
1973	**Margaret Court** In 1973, the US Open became the first Grand Slam tournament to offer equal prize money to male and female winners.
1974	Billie Jean King
1975–78	**Chris Evert** During the 1975 US Open, Evert beat her long-time rival Martina Navratilova in the semi-final. That evening, Navratilova defected to the United States and subsequently won the US Open four times.
1979	Tracy Austin
1980	Chris Evert
1981	Tracy Austin
1982	Chris Evert
1983–84	Martina Navratilova
1985	Hana Mandikova
1986–87	**Martina Navratilova** The four US Open finalists in 1986 (male and female) were all born in Czechoslovakia.
1988–89	Steffi Graf

Things People Did When You Were Growing Up (Part 2)

Finally, here are more of the things we did and errands we ran as kids that nobody needs, wants, or even understands how to do in the modern age!

+ Buy cigarettes for your parents at the corner store as a child
+ Use a pay phone (there was one on almost every corner)
+ Join a bowling league
+ Collect cigarette or baseball trading cards
+ Get frozen meals delivered to your door by the iconic refrigerated yellow Schwan's truck
+ Attend "Lawn Faiths"/ ice cream socials
+ Chat with strangers over CB radio
+ Look up a phone number in the Yellow or White Pages
+ Visit the Bookmobile for new library books
+ Have a radio repaired at an appliance/electronics shop
+ Ride your bike without a helmet
+ Go to American Bandstand parties
+ Take part in a panty raid prank
+ Attend a sock hop
+ Get milk delivered to your door
+ Hang out with friends at a pizzeria
+ Use a rotary phone at home
+ Use a typewriter
+ Save your term paper on a floppy disc
+ Listen to LPs and the newest 45s
+ Care for a pet rock
+ Use a card catalogue to find books at the library
+ Attend a Sadie Hawkins Dance where girls invited the boys
+ Go disco roller skating

Made in the USA
Middletown, DE
04 December 2022

17063671R00066